HOUSTON GOURMET

Cooks & Caterers

by
Ann Criswell

Foreword / Betty Ewing – Columnist Houston Chronicle
Nutrition / Linda McDonald, M.S., R.D., L.D.
Photography & Photo Designer / Ed Daniels
Illustrations / John Bintliff
Design / Larry Knapp

HOUSTON
GOURMET

Publisher / Fran Fauntleroy

Betty Ewing

Bergman and Bogie would have approved these lyrics for "Casablanca" after reading Ann Criswell's latest book, "Houston Gourmet Cooks and Caterers:"

*Now let this truth reveal, a meal's just not a meal
Unless it makes you sighhhhhh,
On Perrier-Jouet you can rely
As time goes by.*

For years now the Houston restaurant/hotel scene has continued to provide a fascinating backdrop for social pageantry. Celebrities and local VIPs and finally Mr. and Mrs. Average Income became a part of the dining-out scene. Super-star chefs started making Houston their destination.

The dining-out pattern spread like a prairie fire, and society columnists observed who was serving what to whom at which buffets.

Back in the 1940s Houston's first gossip columnist, Bill Roberts, of the late (not the new) Houston Press set up his "office" at the then-fabled but now ever-so-defunct Shamrock Hotel. As a prime people-watcher, he reported faithfully on who was dining on spectacular Baked Alaska and French-inspired Vichyssoise as well as which inebriated Epicurean had inhaled a silver pitcher full of ice cubes tossed by an irate band singer.

In 1986, The Chronicle's superb food editor Ann Criswell, by then a veteran connoisseur of viands and vinos, corralled the best restaurants and cooks and compiled their recipes into a sell-out cookbook. Two collections, with Fran Fauntleroy as publisher, have rolled off the presses.

And, as time goes by, Ann now addresses the catering trend. Once a unique service, today the business of cooking and delivering and — if the patron desires — serving, is widespread on the social scene. Anything from pizza to a seven-course dinner for yourself and a few friends at home or an extravaganza for thousands is available.

Houston caterers have interesting track records.

In April, 1981, caterer Hugh Alexander probably set a long-distance catering record. He took a trunk full of Texas barbecued beef and sausage to Monaco for a Western hoedown before Princess Grace's ball to benefit the American Hospital in Paris.

Her serene highness had named longtime friend, Houston socialite Lynn Wyatt, as chairwoman of the Yellow Rose of Texas Ball. Lynn and husband Oscar loaded the Wyatt plane with Texas friends, Chubby Lee's Western Electrik Band and Hugh's barbecue fixings for the hoedown.

Caterer Alexander presented Cutter Bill belt buckles and yellow bandannas to the assisting chefs at the Monte Carlo Sporting Club. They, in turn, presented Hugh with a Texas-shaped cake and a French chorus of "He's a Jolly Good Fellow."

In 1988, caterer Jackson Hicks transported an entire crew, equipment and food to Alberta, Canada, where they laid on 45 separate events during the Winter Olympic Games for a client from New York.

An attractive husband-wife team, Richard and Doreen Kaplan, arrived in Houston from New York a few years ago and set the town on its artistic ear with their Acute Catering.

Top party-givers-on-a-grand-scale, Baron and Baroness di Portanova, called the Kaplans in for their intime dinner party around the pool for UNICEF's international supporter Audrey Hepburn. To salute the film star's memorable Breakfast at Tiffany's Kaplan created a dessert that looked for all the world like a Tiffany box — white chocolate tinted blue and tied with white ribbon. Inside was the dessert, raspberries on satiny white meringue.

New Yorker John Loring, Tiffany's renowned design director, who has at least four books to his credit, was impressed. He ordered a dozen desserts to accompany him to Acapulco where he and a photographer were to record the di Portanovas' legendary mansion, Arabesque, for his new book.

Catering on a far less, yea farrrr less, lavish scale is available. Maybe dinner for six with a two-hour time limit in the cozy familiar confines of your own home.

Here's the scenario:

Old friends telephone that they'll be in town briefly and can stop by your place on the way to the airport. Time is limited, but they can work in a drink and a hunk of cheese. At this point, home is where the heart — but not the food — is.

So what to do in 1990? Call the caterer, says Ann; caterers of abundant talent are in abundant supply.

This year, saluting the remarkable contributions made by restaurants, cooks and caterers to the Houston party scene, the 1990 Criswell edition is titled "Houston Gourmet Cooks and Caterers."

Fran's note: Betty Ewing has been bringing glorious parties and fun social information into our homes via her writing for as long as I can remember. We get to attend the weddings and parties and "travel" through her column. She has brightened many days with fun reading. Thank you, Betty, for making us a part of Houston's changing social scene.

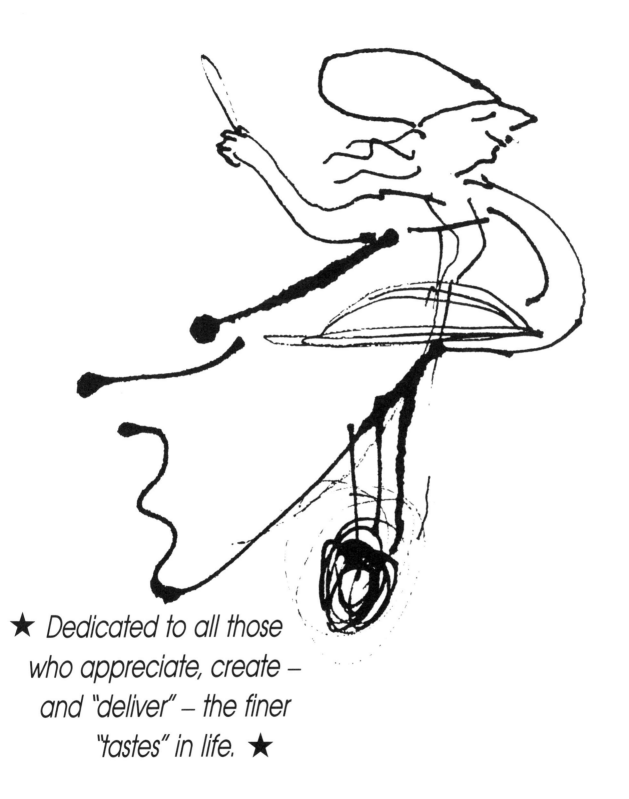

★ *Dedicated to all those who appreciate, create – and "deliver" – the finer "tastes" in life.* ★

Contents ★ ★ ★

Recipes that meet basic health guidelines or can be modified to do so.

Nutrition Tips

Linda McDonald,

M.S., R.D., L.D. Consulting Nutritionist

Restaurateurs and caterers are making changes in the area of nutrition by creating healthy choices that are delicious to look at and to eat.

Choices are what eating is all about and this book is full of choices. If you are concerned about your health or weight, your choices will be based on the nutritional value of the food. But, you also eat for the pleasure that food gives you and this is based on your senses; taste, smell and sight. Food that satisfies your senses can also be healthy.

What does "healthy" really mean? "Healthy" means "good for you". The U. S. Dietary Guidelines for Healthy Americans, the American Heart Association and the American Cancer Society have all given us health guidelines, which basically say:

1) Eat a variety of foods from the four major food groups: Starch/Bread, Fruit/Vegetable, Dairy and Meat/Protein.
2) Eat fat in moderation; not more than 30% of total calories. The American Heart Association also recommends that 10% of total calories should come from saturated fat and not more than 300 milligrams of cholesterol each day.
3) Eat adequate calories to maintain a healthy weight.
4) Limit sodium to about one teaspoon each day, which is approximately 2000 milligrams per day.

The recipes in this book that meet these basic health guidelines or can be modified to do so, are designated with an apple. Suggested recipe modifications are made to meet the basic guidelines listed above without altering the taste or the texture of the product more than necessary. Recipes can be modified in three ways:

1) By changing the amount or eliminating an ingredient.
   Cutting meat portions to 3-6 ounces.
   Omitting salt.
   Reducing sugar or fat.
2) By substituting one ingredient for another.

Instead of:	Use:	Quantity:	Save:	
			Calories	Fat grams
Whole Milk	Skim Milk	1 cup	72	8
Heavy Cream	Half-and-Half	1 cup	506	56
Heavy Cream	Evaporated Skim Milk	1 cup	622	87
Mayonnaise	Light Mayonnaise	1 Tbsp.	60	7
Sour Cream	Yogurt, nonfat	1 cup	366	48
Sour Cream	Buttermilk	1 cup	394	46
Whole Egg	Egg Whites	1	58	10

3) By changing the cooking techniques:
   Broiling or grilling rather than frying.
   Using a non-stick pan for sauteing.
   Spraying pan with non-stick coating spray.
   Skimming off excess fat when making broths.
   Trimming fat off meats.
   Removing skin from poultry.

The nutrient values for all recipes are listed on page 122 & 123 at the end of the book. Recipes that have been modified have two listings, one for the original recipe and one for the modified recipe. Compare this information to decide whether you want, or need to make modifications.

When working with a caterer, don't hesitate to ask about healthy menu suggestions. Many caterers have recipes and menus that are low in fat, calories and sodium or would be willing to modify their recipes.

Ann Criswell

"Houston Gourmet Cooks and Caterers" offers a forecast of the '90s, which one restaurateur describes as the era of the "No Generation" — no smoking, no drinking, no fat, no cholesterol, no fun."

Things may not be that extreme, but we are more concerned about healthful eating, and restaurants and caterers are updating their menus to give diners more options.

Emerging trends include:

* Less cooking from scratch at home. This has given rise to more high-quality take-out and delivery operations, restaurants and caterers. Often our menus are a mixture of home-prepared foods and gourmet-to-go items purchased from a supermarket deli, take-out, restaurant or caterer.

* Eclectic, cross-cultural cooking which blends ethnic foods and cooking styles with fresh regional ingredients — quite often purchased from supermarket delis and caterers.

* Interest in high quality, fresh products that are produced and delivered in environmentally sound ways — organically raised pesticide-free produce; humanely raised animals; safe, degradable, non-polluting packaging/containers, production techniques and waste disposal.

* Renewed interest in fine foods and wines because of increased knowledge of foods and other cultures.

In "Houston Gourmet Cooks and Caterers" you will meet the bright lights of catering in Houston — talented, can-do event planners and cooks who can help build your confidence and reputation as a wonderful host or hostess.

A successful party may be impromptu, but it is seldom an accident. It depends on planning, organization and a charismatic mixture of guests, ambiance, food and service.

Here are some suggestions and comments from the top Houston caterers in this book:

* Look for a caterer who has a good reputation. Personal recommendations from friends or coworkers are better than consulting the Yellow Pages. Ask for recommendations from people who share similar tastes, or, if you are a guest at a good party, find out who catered it.

* Consult the caterer early on and ask for guidance in planning the event. Be honest about your experience, or lack of experience, in planning and hosting parties. But don't be afraid to be specific about things that are important to you; it's your party.

* Telephone first and ask about the caterer's routine. Many caterers have printed information or brochures describing their services. Try to determine from the telephone call if you can establish rapport with the caterer.

* A successful party is financially comfortable. If there are budget restrictions, it is easier to make the party fit the budget than the budget fit the party.

It's bad form to ask a caterer to present a formal proposal if you are "just shopping" for the cheapest price.

Discuss budget candidly and honestly. Caterers can often help you get the best value for your money, or as one Houston caterer puts it colorfully, "the best bang for the bucks."

* Some caterers charge for consultations, especially if the party will be elaborate and require advance expenses such as travel. Often a verbal agreement can be reached on the telephone and the contract can be mailed.

If there is no detailed contract listing specifics on food, services and costs, the client should be wary.

* Reserve the date as soon as possible. The bigger the party, the earlier the caterer should be contacted.

It is not unusual for a caterer to be booked six to eight months in advance, especially for holiday parties, weddings and events that have fixed dates, such as anniversaries or birthdays.

* Primary services are food and staff. Be as specific as possible about what you want; most caterers can arrange for diverse services from invitations to food, flowers, security, valet parking, tenting, music, coat checking and photography.

* Size of the event is not a critical issue, although some caterers require a minimum number of guests. Usually, the smaller the guest list, the more cost-intensive the party is per person. A small party for important people or an important occasion can be as challenging as a large party.

Basic costs for a chef, party manager, planning costs or trucks to transport food and equipment are basically the same whether the party is for six or 60 guests.

* Deposits — it is customary for caterers to require a deposit — usually 50 to 75 percent of the cost — and full payment is expected immediately after the event, just as it is if you entertain in a restaurant or hotel. Some caterers provide limited short-term credit for pre-qualified clients; others break the deposit up in three or four payments, which are due as the work progresses.

* Ask what the caterer's policy is on providing extra food and handling leftover food if more — or fewer — guests show up at the party than have responded to invitations. Most caterers build in some extras. Unused food could perhaps be donated to a food pantry or other End Hunger Network program to help feed the hungry.

Continued on next page

Ann Criswell *continued from previous page*

*Check on progress with the caterer periodically. Be sure the caterer and staff have accurate directions to the party site, are familiar with kitchen and equipment (overloaded electrical systems can spoil the food and plunge the party into darkness), and understand neighborhood security and parking restrictions.

*Give the caterer any special instructions necessary for handling party crashers, smokers, those who have over-imbibed, difficult neighbors and family pets.

About Ann

Ann Criswell, has been food editor of the *Houston Chronicle* since 1966, has written freelance food articles, authored five cookbooks and edited several others.

As food editor of the Chronicle, she contributed most of the recipes in the "Texas the Beautiful Cookbook" published in October, 1986.

She is a member of the Newspaper Food Editors and Writers Association, International Food Media Conference and the Houston Culinary Guild.

In 1987 she was named the first honorary member of the South Texas Dietetic Association and received an award of excellence from the American Heart Association, American Cancer Society and Texas Restaurant Association.

Because of a special interest in wine, she has made several wine tours in Europe and California and has judged Texas wine competitions. She has also judged national cooking contests including the National Beef Cook-Off, National Chicken Cooking Contest and America's Bake-Off.

She is a graduate of Texas Woman's University. Her late husband was a Houston newspaperman and she has a daughter, Catherine, 28, and son, Charles, 26, and a granddaughter, Ryan Criswell, and a grandson, James Lester.

Acknowledgments

Color Separations / Color Technologies Inc.
Typography / C. V. Turner & Assoc.
Printing / Gulf Printing
Basket Design & Balloons / Rice Epicurean Market
Champagne / Perrier-Jouet - Compliments of Chateau and Estate Wines, New York
Glazer's - Houston

Houston Gourmet Cooks & Caterers
Houston, Texas

Printed in the United States of America

ISBN 0-9613643-7-8

Cooks

Calypso

Like a trip to the Caribbean, Calypso restaurant is the mellow, laid-back cure for whatever ails the over-stressed city dweller.

Relaxing with a tropical cooler while ceiling fans turn lazily, exotic fish undulate through aquarium tanks and steeldrum and reggae music pulses with a calming tattoo in the background — you soon discover you've left your troubles at the door.

That's what owners Tim and Jeannie McGann have in mind. They love the Caribbean and wanted to share its lighthearted moods and tantalizing food.

After 10 years of planning, they opened Calypso in 1989 in the Rice University Village. There you can indulge in resort-style cuisine typical of more than 15 Caribbean countries including Jamaica, Barbados, Trinidad, the Dominican Republic, Grenada, St. Maarten, Curacao, Martinique and the Bahamas.

McGann tries to keep the food as authentic as possible — from ingredients to cooking techniques. He brings in the requisite fish and seafood, seasonings, tropical fruits and vegetables and real Key lime juice for the Key Lime Pie.

When substitutions are necessary, he chooses the closest ingredient possible. The popular Calaloo Soup, for example, is made with spinach instead of the leaves of the dasheen plant which are not available. Once mixed with crab, coconut milk, okra and spices, the spinach tastes virtually the same as dasheen.

Star Attractions

★ Carefree atmosphere of a Caribbean island — murals, chairs and table covers in happy tropical prints of pink, turquoise, purple, blue and yellow.

★ Colorful tin-roofed bar is the center of activity, especially during the "Don't Worry, Be Happy Hour" daily from 3:30 to 7 p.m.

★ Saltwater aquariums stocked with a fascinating variety of fish and sea life. The aquariums are maintained by a marine biologist, and the sea life is rotated regularly to create an ever-changing ocean environment.

★ Caribbean bands play music of the islands on weekends — reggae, steel drums, calypso and soca, which resembles salsa.

★ Extensive menu, with more than 30 entrees including Jamaican Jerk chicken and pork dishes such as Tamarind-Apricot Pork Montserrat (grilled pork medallions with an apricot, tamarind and honey sauce). Other specialties: Pitch Lake Cake (Trinidad), conch chowder (the Bahamas) and Shrimp Rellenos (Aruba). The crisply fried curried onions (Grenada) are a must.

★ Authentic ingredients and seasonings showcase the ethnic diversity of the Caribbean— from conch (the conch fritters are one of the city's most unique appetizers), mahi mahi, pompano, grouper and flounder to achiote (an orangish seasoning from the annatto seed), curry, mangos, coconut, Scotch Bonnet peppers, tamarind, black beans and ginger.

★ Extensive bar menu fills eight pages. Twenty-two wines offered by the glass. Domestic and imported beers include Red Stripe beer from Jamaica and Caribe from Trinidad. Coffee drinks such as Jamaican Coffee made with coffee brandy, light rum and coffee. Specialty rum drinks include:

Feel No Way Punch invented by general manager Bill Stender. A frozen drink, it is a blend of three rums, four tropical fruit juices, grenadine and spices;

Jeannie's Wavecutter — Gold rum, cranberry juice and orange juice; Duppy (the Caribbean term for ghost) blends rum, hazelnut, cream de cacao, orange juice and half-and-half; Charlotte Amalie, a secret blend of light, dark and 151 rums with citrus; Goombay Smash — dark rum, coconut rum, pineapple, lemon and Triple Sec.

Calypso probably has the largest selection of fine rums north of Havana including Barbencourt Fifteen Year Old Rhum, which many guests enjoy as an after-dinner drink because it is as smooth as brandy.

★ Catering — from selected take-out items to complete parties with serving boat, sand and sea shells, tiki torches, Caribbean bands and flowers with full-service waiters and bartenders.

★ Daily lunch specials.

★ Sunday brunch of Caribbean specialties.

★ Continuous service daily from 11:30 a.m. to 10 p.m. Monday through Wednesday; to 11 p.m. Thursday and Sunday; to midnight, Friday and Saturday. The bar is open until 2 a.m. Friday and Saturday.

★ Private parties. Although there are no private rooms, small groups can be accommodated in the partially walled lounge area.

Kahlua Banana Colada

1	ounce rum
½	ounce Kahlua
½	ounce banana liqueur
½	medium banana, cut in chunks
½	ounce canned cream of coconut
2	ounces pineapple juice
2	ounces half-and-half
	Dash of unsweetened cocoa powder
	Pineapple slice, maraschino cherry and small paper parasol for garnish

Combine rum, Kahlua, liqueur, banana, cream of coconut, pineapple juice, half-and-half and cocoa powder in electric blender. Blend until smooth. Serve in a hurricane glass and garnish with pineapple slice, cherry and paper parasol favor.

Serves 1.

Gingered Chicken with Mango

4 (8-ounce) boneless, skinless chicken breasts
   Flour
4 tablespoons peanut oil, heated
2 cups peeled, diced ripe mangos
½ cup dark brown sugar
½ teaspoon fresh ground cloves
4 teaspoons peeled, grated fresh ginger
1 teaspoon soy sauce

Dredge chicken in flour and saute in hot oil in a skillet over medium heat. When brown, 4 to 5 minutes, remove from pan and keep warm. Wipe skillet clean. Combine mangos, brown sugar, cloves, ginger and soy sauce. Cook in skillet over medium heat 1 to 2 minutes. Top chicken with mixture and serve.

Serve with rice, black beans and fried ripe plantains.

Serves 4.

🍎 Good recipe for healthy eating. Divide the recipe into eight servings instead of four, for a chicken portion of 3.5 ounces.

Jerk Pork

8   (5-ounce) center cut pork chops (or pork loin or tenderloin) or 4 (8-ounce) boneless, skinless chicken breasts
25 to 30 whole black peppercorns, ground
15 whole allspice berries, ground
1   medium white onion, chopped (about 1 cup)
1   cup chopped scallions (white part only)
4   tablespoons fresh Jamaican thyme, chopped (see Note)
2   Scotch bonnet peppers, chopped (see Note)
2   tablespoons Worcestershire sauce
2   tablespoons bottled liquid smoke
    Salt as needed
1   tablespoon sugar
4   tablespoons vegetable oil
1   tablespoon minced garlic
1   tablespoon ground cinnamon
½   cup chopped green onion tops

Combine ground peppercorns, allspice, onion, scallions, thyme, peppers, Worcestershire, liquid smoke, salt, sugar, oil, garlic and cinnamon in a food processor and process until a loose paste forms. Remove and put in a saucepan. Add the green onion tops and heat until onion wilts. Remove from heat and cool.

Rub into pork and marinate in the refrigerator overnight.

Remove pork from marinade and cook over hard wood coals until done; do not overcook.

Serves 4.

Note: Available in Caribbean markets.

🍎 Use lean pork loin; reduce oil to 4 teaspoons for a low-fat entree.

Peanut Butter Pie

This dessert is one of the most popular on the menu. Tim McGann's mother passed it along to him.

Crust
3	cups all-purpose flour
1	teaspoon salt
1	cup solid all-vegetable shortening
⅜	cup milk

Combine flour and salt. Cut in shortening with pastry blender until the size of coarse cornmeal. Add half the milk all at once, then add more gradually until dough is wet enough to hold together without being sticky.

Divide in half. Reserve half for future use (freezes well). Roll dough into a ball. Roll dough out slightly larger than a 9-inch pie plate between sheets of plastic wrap (dampening counter with a wet sponge will help keep bottom piece of wrap from sliding).

Remove top piece of wrap and turn dough into pie plate. When centered, remove wrap and crimp edges. Pierce dough all over with a fork. Bake at 350 degrees until brown, about 10 to 12 minutes.

Filling
1	cup powdered sugar
½	cup creamy peanut butter
2	cups milk
⅔	cup granulated sugar
3	tablespoons cornstarch
	Dash of salt
3	egg yolks, lightly beaten
¼	teaspoon vanilla
1	cup whipping cream

Mix powdered sugar and peanut butter in food processor and process until crumbly. Spread two-thirds of mixture in baked pie shell. Set remaining third aside for topping/garnish.

Heat milk in saucepan until warm. In small bowl, combine granulated sugar, cornstarch and salt. Beat in egg yolks. Whisk in a little of the warm milk. Mix well, then add this mixture to remaining milk in pan. Cook, whisking, until thick and bubbly. Cool slightly; add vanilla.

Pour over peanut-sugar mixture. Whip cream (chill cream, bowl and beaters well before whipping). Cover top of pie with whipped cream and sprinkle rest of peanut-sugar mixture over top. Refrigerate several hours before serving.

Note: Pie can be made ahead and refrigerated and whipped cream added just before serving.

Calypso
5555 Morningside #100
Houston, Texas 77005
524-8571

Cavatore

An Italian restaurant in an old Texas barn may seem incongruous, but the marriage of Italian food and a 100-year-old barn has been a successfully happy one for Cavatore.

The barn was taken apart, piece by piece, and moved from a rustic setting in Bastrop, Texas, to Ella Boulevard just east of Loop 610. It is only minutes from the Galleria, downtown, River Oaks, the Heights and Northwest Mall. It is across the street from the owners' other restaurant, La Tour d'Argent, a French restaurant housed in an old log cabin (see Page 28).

Cavatore's coat of arms is more than 800 years old and comes from a small medieval village in northern Italy, an area famous for truffles and some of Italy's most prestigious wines.

The restaurant's emblem is a stylized blend of American, Italian and Texas flags and Texas' five-pointed Lone Star. The emblem appears in stained glass windows, on waiters' aprons and matchbook covers.

Written in Italian with English translations, the menu is quintessentially Italian — antipasto such as fried mozzarella cheese and fried squid; pasta including Fettuccine Alfredo, Spaghetti Bolognese and Linguini With Clams; grilled chicken, fish and seafood such as Shrimp Marinara; classic veal dishes — Marsala, Parmigiana, Piccata — and desserts such as cannoli, spumoni and cheesecake.

Rebuilt and restored as closely as possible to its original state, the barn has wooden floors and walls and sheet metal ceiling. At one point to get enough sheet metal to preserve the ceiling's authenticity, partner Sonny Lahham said he even advertised in the newspaper for rusty sheet metal.

Memorabilia that covers the walls — original movie posters, family photographs, mementos and vintage newspapers — were found by advertising in a newspaper in Milan, Italy, home of partner Giancarlo Cavatore's mother.

The menu cover is a conversation piece — a colorful cartoon map of Columbus sailing toward America with a boat load of foodstuffs. Photos of historic figures, family, friends and even family pets are worked into the scene.

Star Attractions

★ Setting—"The oldest barn in Houston" with a fascinating array of memorabilia, photographs, stained glass windows, baskets, fresh flowers and plants.

★ Wine room for private parties; seats 12.

★ Convivial setting for office and business luncheons, dinner and special occasions or just meeting a friend for a drink. Accommodations for private parties.

★ Outside deck with umbrella tables.

★ Small kitchen garden where fresh herbs and vegetables are grown.

★ Live piano music every night except Sundays.

★ Tableside food preparation; two specials daily are prepared at the table.

★ Wine list with more than 100 selections; good choices from Italy (especially the fine wines of the Piedmont area), France and California.

★ Dessert tray; espresso, cappuccino and dessert coffee.

Peperonata

- 1   **eggplant, sliced**
- 1   **zucchini, sliced**
- ½   **cup (or less to taste) extra-virgin olive oil**
- 3   **garlic cloves, chopped**
- ¼   **each: green, red and yellow bell peppers, diced**
  Chopped fresh basil and salt and pepper (optional)

Saute sliced eggplant and zucchini in 2 tablespoons of the olive oil until they are cooked. Combine with garlic and peppers, top with remaining olive oil and chill about 2 hours before serving. If desired, add chopped fresh basil, salt and pepper. Serve as an appetizer, dip or spread with crackers or thin rounds of French bread.

Serves 4.

Decrease olive oil to ¼ cup to cut fat calories in half. Serve with plain toast for a healthy appetizer. The nutrient analysis is for eight, ½ cup servings, plus five melba toast.

Spinach Soup with Egg Drop (Stracciatella)

- ½   **pound fresh spinach, washed and well cleaned**
- 2   **cups chicken broth**
  Salt and pepper
- 1   **egg white**
- 2   **tablespoons grated cheese**

Cook the fresh spinach until limp with just the water clinging to the leaves. Strain and squeeze all water out. Add chicken broth with salt and pepper (if needed) and let come to a boil. Stir in egg white. Remove from heat. Before serving, top with grated cheese.

Serves 2 to 4.

Deliciously healthy way to get lots of vitamin A and C without much fat.

Veal Milanese

6 ounces thinly sliced veal tenderloin, pounded thin
2 eggs, lightly beaten
   Seasoned bread crumbs
   Salt and pepper (optional)
1 tablespoon olive oil
   Lemon (optional)

Dip veal slices in beaten egg, then in bread crumbs (salt and pepper if needed) covering well. Saute in a little olive oil in a skillet. Squeeze lemon on top before serving, if desired.

Serves 1 to 2.

🍎 Fix this for two. Dip veal in egg substitute to cut cholesterol. Spray non-stick skillet with coating spray; use one teaspoon of olive oil.

Fettuccine Cavatore

1 pound fettuccine
   Olive oil
4 garlic cloves, diced
2 green onions, chopped
1 sun-dried tomato
2 fresh tomatoes
½ pound each: calamari (see Note) and shrimp, peeled and deveined
   Salt and pepper
10 fresh sweet basil leaves, coarsely chopped

Cook fettuccine al dente (firm to the tooth) in large pot of boiling, salted water adding 1 tablespoon oil. Drain.

In another pan, saute garlic and green onion until garlic turns golden. Add sun-dried tomato and fresh tomatoes and let simmer about 10 minutes. In the meantime, saute shrimp and calamari. Add to the tomato sauce with chopped basil. Pour sauce over a bed of fettuccine.

Note: To clean calamari:
Wash thoroughly under cold running water. Cut off tentacles; run finger down inside then pull insides out through mouth. Squeeze excess fluid out of the ink sac. Cut off and discard the mouth.

Wash again under cold running water; cut into ½-inch rings.

Serves 4.

🍎 This dish is high in cholesterol, but low in fat. Omit oil in pasta; use only 1 tablespoon oil to saute vegetables and 1 tablespoon oil to saute seafood.

Scallops with Lemon

12   ounces sea scallops
      Flour
2   to 3 tablespoons butter, melted
2   garlic cloves, minced
2   teaspoons minced fresh parsley
4   fresh sweet basil leaves, coarsely chopped
1   teaspoon fresh lemon juice
2   ounces (4 tablespoons) white wine
      Salt and pepper

Dip scallops in flour, then saute in 2 or 3 tablespoons melted butter about 3 minutes. Add garlic, parsley and basil and cook 1 more minute. Add lemon juice and wine and let simmer about 2 minutes. Do not overcook. Add salt and pepper.

Serves 2.

Use only one tablespoon margarine for sauteing.

Cavatore Italian Restaurant
2120 Ella Boulevard
Houston, Texas 77008
869-6622

Fu's Garden

Fu's Garden opened New Year's Eve in 1989, but it is already a landmark destination in the Rice University Village for devotees of Chinese — particularly Hunan—cuisine.

Owner George Fu, who came from Chinese Cambodia, is an experienced restauranteur who trained in Los Angeles. He owned several other Chinese restaurants in Houston, Bellaire and Clear Lake (including Fen Ling) before buying Fu's Garden. Another Fu's Garden is scheduled to open in October, 1990, at 5866 San Felipe.

Fu's Garden offers the traditional Chinese dishes, but specializes in healthful, fresh ingredients prepared to order without excess fat and fillers.

A setting of subtle elegance is created with restful shades of taupe, mauve, plum, burgundy and rosy pink, handsome furnishings, fresh flowers on each table and Oriental screens imported from Taiwan. The largest screen about 20 feet long, depicts peace and happiness. Highly polished rosewood chairs with claret-red velvet cushions underscore custom-designed table tops; each has a charming Chinese scene laminated on it.

Star Attractions

★ Located in the Rice University Village, convenient to the Texas Medical Center, Astrodome, Summit and downtown.

★ Traditional dishes such as Pork Steamed Dumplings, Tea-Smoked Chicken, Hot and Sour Soup, Wonton Soup, Kung Pao Chicken, Sweet and Sour Pork, Beef with Broccoli, several varieties of fried rice and lo mein (soft noodles).

★ Chef Fu's specialties: Orange Flavor Hot Beef, Hot Shredded Szechuan Pork, Pan Fried Chinese Bacon, Kung Pao Shrimp, Hunan softshell crab, whole fish and bean curd dishes.

★ Family dinners for two or more with choice of soup, appetizers and entrees.

★ Luncheon specials served daily from 11:30 a.m. to 3 p.m. Choice of soup, fried rice, spring roll and entrees.

★ Diet dishes including Four Flavors of Fresh Cooked Vegetables, Chicken Tenders with Broccoli and Sliced Fish With Mixed Vegetables.

★ Hot and spicy dishes indicated on menu by stars. Each dish is cooked fresh to order; spiciness is adjusted on request. Also will substitute ingredients to create dishes to order.

★ Full-service bar.

★ Open daily for lunch and dinner. Extended hours: Monday through Thursday, 11:30 a.m. to 10 p.m.; Friday, 11:30 a.m. to midnight; Saturday, noon to midnight; Sunday, noon to 10 p.m.

★ Take-out; free home delivery within five miles (minimum order $15).

Sauteed Chicken with Peppercorn Sauce

- 1 **pound boneless white meat of chicken, cut in chunks**
- 1 **egg white**
- 1 **tablespoon cornstarch**
- 3 **cups vegetable oil**
- ½ **cup sliced winter bamboo shoots (see Note)**
- ½ **cup each: chopped green and red bell peppers**
- 2 **teaspoons Chinese hot red pepper paste**
- 1 **teaspoon each: chopped garlic and peeled, chopped fresh ginger**
- ½ **teaspoon ground Chinese peppercorns (see Note)**
- 1 **tablespoon soy sauce**
- ½ **teaspoon salt (optional)**
- 1 **teaspoon sugar**
- 2 **teaspoons cornstarch dissolved in 2 tablespoons chicken broth**
- 1 **tablespoon white wine**
- 1 **teaspoon each: sesame oil and vinegar**

Stir egg white, add chicken and stir in cornstarch; mix well. Marinate chicken in mixture while heating oil to 350 degrees in wok. Quickly stir-fry chicken 30 seconds. Add bamboo shoots and peppers and stir-fry 30 seconds. Drain oil, and set food aside.

Reheat wok, add hot pepper paste, chopped garlic, ginger and ground peppercorns; saute 5 seconds. Add chicken mixture, mix well and saute with sauce (mixture of soy sauce, salt, sugar, dissolved cornstarch and wine. Splash sesame oil and vinegar over dish. Stir and Serve.

Serves 4.

Notes: Winter bamboo shots are finer, crisper and more expensive than regular bamboo shoots. Chinese peppercorns resemble small seed pods and have a distinctive aromatic fragrance when ground.

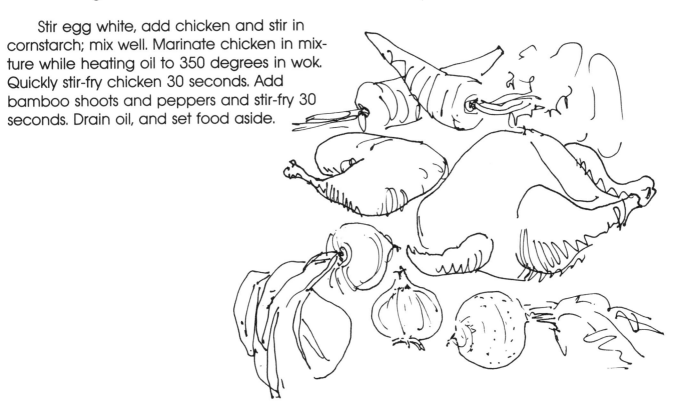

Sauteed Baby Shrimp with Cashews

1   pound medium baby shrimp, cleaned, peeled and deveined (if fresh unavailable, use frozen shrimp)
1   egg white
1   tablespoon cornstarch
3   cups vegetable oil
1   teaspoon salt (optional)
½   teaspoon sugar
¼   teaspoon ground white pepper
1   teaspoon white wine
½   cup fried cashews (see Note)
1   cup snow peas, blanced quickly in boiling water
½   teaspoon wine vinegar
1   teaspoon sesame oil

Keep shrimp in ice water until cleaned, then drain well. Stir egg white, add shrimp, then stir in cornstarch; marinate shrimp in refrigerator about 20 minutes.

Heat oil in wok to 400 degrees, add shrimp and stir quickly 20 seconds. Remove from wok; drain oil. Reheat wok over low temperature. Add 1 teaspoon oil, salt, sugar and pepper. Return shrimp, fried cashews and snow peas to wok; mix well. Splash vinegar and sesame oil over dish before serving.

Serves 4 if having other dishes.

Note: To fry cashews: Heat 1 cup oil to 100 degrees. Add cashews and heat slowly to 300 degrees, until cashews turn light brown. Do not let them get too brown. Drain and set aside.

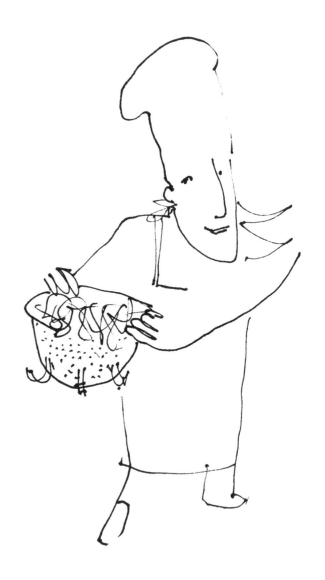

Steamed Salmon with Fresh Vegetables

10   ounces fresh salmon fillets, sliced about ½-inch thick
1   to 2 cups mixed fresh vegetables such as fresh mushrooms, broccoli and cauliflower florets, snow peas, carrots, baby corn and Napa cabbage, cleaned and trimmed
1   tablespoon each: pineapple sauce (see Notes), applesauce, Hoisin sauce, vinegar, light soy sauce and plum sauce

Clean vegetables, cut in bite-size pieces or slices and drop into a small amount of rapidly boiling water; blanch 5 seconds; drain.

Set a plate in stainless steel steamer, arrange bed of vegetables on plate and top with salmon. Steam 1 minute; salmon should be pale pink and vegetables should be crisp-tender.

Serve with sauce made by mixing pineapple sauce, applesauce, Hoisin, vinegar, soy sauce and plum sauce.

Serves 2 or more depending on number of other dishes served.

Notes: If you don't have a steamer, vegetables can be cooked crisp-tender in a small amount of boiling water, and salmon can be poached — don't overcook or fish will fall apart.

If canned pineapple sauce is not available, puree crushed pineapple in blender until smooth.

This recipe is low-fat — only 30 percent of calories come from fat. Use low sodium soy sauce.

Sauteed Green Beans with Ground Meat

1   pound fresh green beans
5   cups cooking oil
1   ounce cooked ground meat (beef or pork)
1   ounce finely chopped canned Chinese pickle (see Note)
1   teaspoon chopped garlic
1   tablespoon each: soy sauce and sugar
½   teaspoon salt
¼   teaspoon ground white pepper
1   teaspoon sesame oil

Trim off both ends of beans. Carefully heat oil to 450 degrees in deep fryer. Lower beans into oil in a fry basket and deep-fry beans 15 seconds. Drain thoroughly. Reheat wok with a little oil and saute ground meat and pickle until dry, about 30 seconds.

Add chopped garlic, soy sauce, sugar, salt, white pepper, sesame oil and beans; stir quickly until well mixed.

Serves 4.

Notes: No cornstarch is required for thickening. Be very careful when heating oil and lowering beans into it; oil should be very hot so beans will cook almost instantly and won't absorb oil. Chinese pickle is a salty preserved pickle available in Asian markets.

General Tip: Use low-sodium soy sauce; omit salt; use oil in moderation; serve with plain boiled rice.

Fu's Garden
2539 University Blvd.
Houston, Texas 77005
520-7422

Jack's on Woodway

Exciting things are coming from the kitchen of Jack's on Woodway, another success for veteran restaurateur Jack Ray.

The restaurant, done in painted desert colors, tile, stucco and terra cotta provides a fitting background for the creative Southwestern-style cooking of chef Peter Zimmer.

Black beans, wood-grilled vegetables, blue corn tortillas, tomatillos, chilies, pepper jellies, salsas and cactus chutney play their part in defining the Southwestern culinary boundaries. So do architectural features such as the adobe beehive fireplace in the bar.

But the menu goes farther to feature fresh regional foods, Gulf Coast seafood and fish, pasta, wild game, beef and such dishes as hot-ash roasted pork loin wrapped in banana leaves with cinnamon-chile crust.

The emphasis is on healthful cooking; a heart symbol marks heart-smart, low-sodium, low-fat dishes on the menu.

Star Attractions

★ Convenient location just west of Loop 610 for after-work get togethers in the comfortable bar, dinner after shopping in the Galleria or early dinner on the way to a downtown theater or concert.

★ Innovative Southwestern cuisine by an up-and-coming young chef, Peter Zimmer, whose mentors include Wolfgang Puck and celebrated regional chef Dean Fearing of The Mansion on Turtle Creek in Dallas.

★ Signature dishes — Black Bean Soup, Cajeta Black Bean Crepes with Pan Seared Vegetables; Stuffed Free-Range Chicken with Grilled Squash Salad; Honey Roasted Quail with Sweet Corn Cilantro Sauce; Broiled Catfish with Grilled Corn Hushpuppies, and Jack's Sack, a decadent dessert. A molded sack of hard chocolate is filled with a layer of cake, chocolate mousse, fresh berries and Grand Marnier cream nested on a caramel sauce.

The chef also is known for specialties cooked on the wood-burning grill and flavorings such as infused oils from tamarind, chipotle peppers, fruits and herbs; he uses them for seasonings with aged vinegars.

★ Wild game — Jack's specializes in cooking and preparing game from rattlesnake to elk and wild boar. Zimmer will prepare customers' game for private parties and caters wild game dinners at the restaurant and in homes.

★ Catering — Private parties and charity benefits for groups of 30 to 500 on or off the premises. Jack's has catered wedding receptions, a square-dance, chuckwagon and other theme parties. The restaurant can provide only the food or handle everything from service, flowers and entertainment to ice carvings.

★ Can screen off bar and adjacent dining area for private parties.

★ Home delivery of catering items from Jalapeno Cream Cheese Soup for 50 to hors d'oeuvres for 500.

★ Appealing decor that takes its cue from New Mexico and Arizona. Decorating touches include paintings (most are from galleries in Santa Fe and Taos) in painted frames that are works of art themselves; a painted faux rug floor, carved tables, pottery vases and urns and painted wooden snakes.

★ Desserts made on the premises such as Baked Feuilletee with Peaches and Cream (puff pastry with fresh peaches), Mexican Nut Tart and homemade ice cream.

Frozen Coyote is the house dessert drink — rum, Midori melon liqueur and pineapple juice.

Baby Leaf Greens with Achiote-Fried Oysters and Papaya Roasted Coriander Vinaigrette

- 1 **dozen fresh oysters, shucked (or 2 jars refrigerated oysters)**
- 1 **tablespoon roasted coriander seeds**
- ½ **tablespoon (1½ teaspoons) chopped garlic**
- 1 **bunch cilantro, cleaned and patted dry**
- 1 **tablespoon each: honey and lime juice**
- 2 **papayas, cleaned and seeded**
- ½ **teaspoon cayenne pepper**
  Salt and pepper
  Cold pressed, extra-virgin olive oil (Gondola or Colavita brands preferred)
- ½ **cup each: all-purpose flour and cornmeal**
- ½ **teaspoon cayenne pepper**
- 1 **tablespoon achiote (yellow seasoning derived from the annatto tree) or paprika**
- 1 **whole radicchio**
- 1 **dozen each: Mezuna greens or watercress, arugula leaves and baby red oak lettuce leaves**
- 6 **whole Belgian endive**

In blender or food processor combine roasted coriander, garlic, cilantro, honey, lime juice and chunks of papaya. Puree on high. Add cayenne, salt and pepper. Slowly add 1 cup olive oil in a thin, steady stream through the blender cap until mixture thickens to a loose mayonnaise.

To roast coriander seeds, place seeds in a single layer on a sheet pan and roast 3 minutes at 425 degrees.

Combine flour, cornmeal, cayenne and achiote. Dust oysters with this mixture. Heat 2 tablespoons olive oil in large skillet and flash-fry oysters.

Arrange mixture of lettuces and endive on 4 plates; drizzle with papaya vinaigrette and top with oysters.

Serves 4.

Use 1 tablespoon oil for sauteing oysters; ½ cup oil in papaya vinaigrette and 2 tablespoons of vinaigrette per serving.

Grilled Tiger Prawns with Yellow Tomatoes and Artichokes

½   tablespoon (1½ teaspoons) olive oil
12   tiger prawns or jumbo shrimp, cleaned with heads on
1   teaspoon minced garlic
½   cup sliced red onion
1   cup cooked sliced bacon, crumbled
2   cups small, whole yellow tear-drop shaped tomatoes
2   cups well-cleaned fresh spinach
½   cup balsamic vinegar
½   cup sweet sherry
     Salt, pepper and cayenne pepper
¼   cup mixed chopped fresh Italian parsley and basil
3   bunches arugula, cleaned and patted dry
4   artichoke bottoms
     Italian parsley sprigs for garnish

Heat oil in large saute pan; cook prawns until almost done, about 2 minutes. Add garlic, onion, bacon, tomatoes and spinach; saute 2 minutes. Deglaze pan with vinegar and sherry (stir in and quickly scrape up any drippings as liquid evaporates).

Add salt, pepper, cayenne to taste, chopped parsley and basil. Place arugula and an artichoke bottom on each of 4 (8-inch) plates and spoon mixture over top. Arrange 3 prawns in a nest on top of warm salad. Garnish with Italian parsley.

Serves 4.

🍎 Good, healthy recipe. Omit bacon to cut fat calories.

Pecan Wood-Grilled Lamb Loin with Grilled Trumpet Mushrooms and Whole Grain Honey Mustard

4   (3-ounce) boneless pecan wood-grilled lamb loins
12   large trumpet mushrooms, shiitake or brown mushrooms, grilled
½   cup whole-grain mustard
½   cup fresh lime juice
½   cup honey
2   egg yolks
1   cup peanut oil
1   bunch cilantro, chopped
1   tablespoon cider vinegar
     Salt, pepper and cayenne

In mixing bowl or food processor, combine mustard, lime juice, honey and egg yolks. With motor running, slowly add peanut oil through feed tube until mixture is the consistency of loose mayonnaise. Stir in cilantro, vinegar, salt, pepper and cayenne to taste.

Ladle honey mustard over a 10-inch plate to cover. Slice the lamb and fan it out on mustard sauce. Arrange mushrooms at top of plate. Garnish with cilantro leaves.

Serves 4.

🍎 Use ½ cup egg substitute for egg yolks; only 2 ounces peanut oil; omit salt.

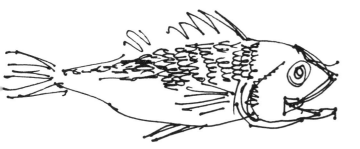

Mahi Baked in Paper with Grilled Chanterelles

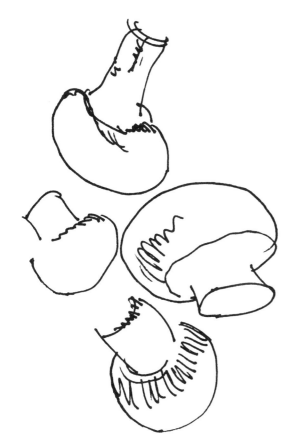

4   sheets parchment paper (see Notes)
4   (6-ounce) fillets of mahi mahi
1   cup cooked cavitopi pasta (corkscrew tube pasta)
2   cups grilled chanterelle mushrooms
1   cup sliced leeks (white part only)
1   teaspoon chopped garlic
½   cup mixed chopped fresh Italian parsley and Mexican mint marigold or tarragon
     Salt, white pepper and cayenne
2   tablespoons butter
½   cup whole sundried tomatoes
½   cup lobster stock, fish stock or clam juice (see Notes)

Lay 4 sheets of parchment paper on work space. Place one-fourth of the cooked pasta, mushrooms, leeks, garlic, parsley, mint marigold and a pinch each of salt, pepper and cayenne in center of each.

Divide butter in 4 equal parts; place in center of paper. Place raw fish on top and sundried tomatoes inside the pasta. Ladle lobster stock over top of fish. Pick up corners of parchment paper and twist to form a bag. Fold toward center on baking sheet. Bake at 425 degrees 15 to 20 minutes

Serves 4.

Notes: Parchment paper is available at gourmet, food specialty shops and fine super-markets. Aluminum foil may be substituted. Fish stock bases are available in better super-markets (Minor's and Knorr's are two brands).

🍎 An innovative way to cook low-fat; fish stays moist and flavorful with little added fat.

Jack's on Woodway
5055 Woodway
Houston, Texas 77056
623-0788

La Tour d'Argent

Chef Hassni Malla trained under French, German and Swiss chefs and worked in Paris, Spain and elsewhere in Europe before he came to the United States as chef for the Warwick (now the Wyndham Warwick). He helped open the Westin Galleria, was chef at the former Biscayne and owned the Vendome restaurant in Conroe from 1986 to 1988. He joined La Tour in 1989.

R omantic atmosphere and classic French food combine to make dining at La Tour d'Argent an unforgettable experience

The restaurant, a log cabin with hunting lodge decor on the wooded banks of White Oak Bayou east of Loop 610, could serve as a movie set. Walls are almost concealed by hunting trophies — more than 2,000 mounted deer antlers, moose, elk and even rhinoceros heads — as well as lion and tiger skins.

The log cabin was built in 1917 and is the oldest log cabin in Houston. It was almost destroyed by fire just as it was being readied to open as a restaurant in 1981. One of the owners, Sonny Lahham, his wife and friends rented a sand blaster and scraped and renovated the burned logs one by one, and the restaurant opened only slightly behind schedule.

The romantic atmosphere is enhanced by leaded glass doors and windows, stone fireplaces, wooden tongue-in-groove floors and wood-beamed ceiling, master paintings and antiques of collector quality, hand-carved reproductions of Queen Anne chairs, fine china and fresh flowers — usually red roses — on the tables.

In keeping with the hunting lodge theme, the menu often features game such as buffalo, venison, wild boar, elk and game birds.

La Tour d'Argent is known as much for its fine French cuisine and wine cellar as its unique setting. It has earned the Mobil Travel Guide four-star award and has been widely recognized for its cuisine and exceptional wine list.

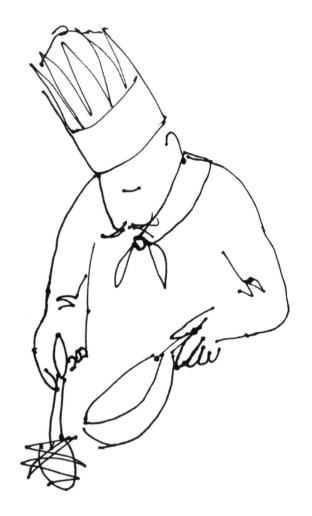

Star Attractions

★ French cuisine — one of the few traditional French restaurants in Houston.

★ Appealing setting and atmosphere for power lunches, business meetings, dinner to impress the boss or a date, or just to while away rainy hours over a bottle of wine with someone special.

★ Alcoves and rooms for secluded dining including the Garden Room that overlooks a gazebo, two man-made waterfalls and a small stream where ducks and geese glide by.

★ The resident wildlife — quail, raccoons, rabbits, squirrels and birds (including a cage of pigeons, doves and pheasant in the Crocodile Room), provide continuing entertainment for diners.

★ Excellent and extensive wine list — particularly strong in French and California listings. The wine loft (available for small parties or tastings) stores 1,200 cases of wine. Wines dating to 1753 on display; drinkable vintages dating to 1898.

★ Polished, professional service.

★ Harpist plays for special occasions.

Shrimp Gratin (Gratin de Crevettes)

12   **jumbo shrimp, peeled and deveined**
¼   **pound fresh mushrooms, sliced**
2   **teaspoons shallots, peeled and finely chopped**
2   **teaspoons butter**
½   **cup grated swiss cheese**
    White Wine Sauce (recipe follows)

Saute the mushrooms and shallots in 1 teaspoon butter or olive oil in a hot skillet; drain off liquid. Divide mushroom mixture between 2 ovenproof plates.

Saute shrimp in remaining butter in skillet until they turn pink; do not overcook. Arrange around mushrooms. Top with swiss cheese and place plate in 325-degree oven until cheese melts, about 3 minutes. When melted, remove from oven and pour white wine sauce on top. Garnish with a basil leaf or chopped parsley or dill.

Serves 2.

White Wine Sauce
½   **cup white wine**
½   **cup fish stock**
¼   **cup heavy (whipping) cream, half-and-half or skim milk**
    Salt and pepper as needed

Heat a skillet; add wine and fish stock and let simmer 2 minutes. Whisk in cream and salt and pepper to taste and let simmer until thick.

🍎 Use 2 ounces cheese; substitute evaporated skim milk for cream.

Cold Cream of Asparagus and Avocado

½ **pound fresh asparagus, trimmed and cooked**
2 **teaspoons butter**
2 **teaspoons chopped onion**
2 **teaspoons chopped celery**
2 **cups chicken stock**
2 **cups heavy (whipping) cream, half-and-half or skim milk**
　 Salt and pepper
½ **avocado, peeled and diced**

Cook asparagus until very soft in boiling water (see Note). Drain and puree smooth in blender or food processor. Heat butter in a 1 to 1½-quart saucepan and saute onion and celery until limp.

Add asparagus and chicken stock; let simmer until mixture is reduced by one-fourth. Remove from heat and let cool, about 10 minutes. Blend in cream, salt and pepper and stir in diced avocado.

Serves 2.

Note: Can cook asparagus in microwave with a few tablespoons water, covered, on high power until soft, about 6 minutes.

🍎 Omit butter; substitute evaporated skim milk for cream, and you cut 45 grams of fat per serving.

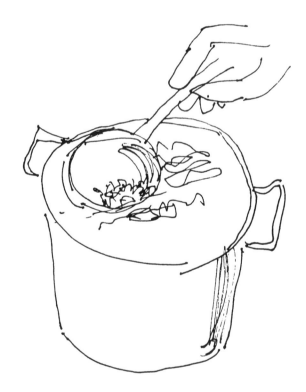

Chicken with Mustard

4   **whole boneless chicken breasts**
      Flour
1   **tablespoon butter**
1   **teaspoon chopped shallots**
¼   **pound fresh mushrooms, sliced**
¼   **cup dry white wine**
¼   **cup chicken stock**
¼   **cup whipping cream, half-and-half or skim milk**
1   **tablespoon Dijon mustard**

Dust chicken with flour. Heat butter in a skillet and saute chicken breasts until golden brown, about 7 to 10 minutes. Remove chicken from pan. Add shallots, mushrooms, wine, stock and cream to same pan. Add mustard and cream and let sauce simmer until it is reduced by one-fourth. Return chicken to pan and simmer about 2 minutes.

When cooked, place a portion of mushrooms on top of each chicken breast and pour mustard sauce over all.

Serves 4.

🍎 Use half-and-half and percent of calories from fat drops below 30 per cent.

Veal Scallops Armagnac (Escalopes de Veau Armagnac)

¼   **pound fresh mushrooms, sliced**
2   **ounces (4 tablespoons) butter**
1   **pound veal tenders, sliced about ¼-inch thick and pounded flat (1½-ounces per scallop)**
      Flour, salt and pepper
1   **cup veal stock**
½   **cup heavy (whipping) cream**
2   **ounces Armagnac brandy**
1   **teaspoon chopped shallots**

Melt a little butter in a skillet and saute mushrooms; drain off any extra liquid. Set mushrooms aside. Dust veal scallops with flour seasoned with salt and pepper. Melt remaining butter and saute veal in hot skillet until light brown, about 1 to 2 minutes. Add shallots and cook until light golden color. Add Armagnac, veal stock and cream and let cook until reduced to a sauce. Return mushrooms to pan and let heat through.

To serve, arrange three veal scallops on each plate. Top with one-fourth of the mushrooms and spoon sauce over them.

Serves 4.

🍎 Substitute evaporated skim milk for cream; use 1 tablespoon margarine; use lean veal.

La Tour d'Argent
2011 Ella Blvd. & T.C. Jester
Houston, Texas 77008
864-9864

Rainbow Lodge

Rainbow Lodge offers contemporary American cuisine in a setting right out of the pages of a romance novel.

Located on the wooded banks of Buffalo Bayou, the Lodge is surrounded by a two-acre park-like expanse of manicured grounds. A footbridge over a man-made pond and waterfall ringed with flowers leads to a gazebo. It is the setting for 75 to 100 weddings throughout the year, sometimes three on a busy Saturday.

Ducks waddle about the grounds and swim in the pond, but the real attention-getters are three plastic gooseblinds that look like giant Canadian geese.

During the Christmas holidays thousands of twinkle lights adorn the trees.

If the building seems like a home, it is because it was built as a one-story residence in the 1930s. It was remodeled in the late 1970s as a rustic, multilevel hunting lodge. The eclectic mix of antiques, hunting and fishing trophies, purple cedar tree-trunk railings on the stairs, polished wooden floors, leaded glass doors, tapestry fabrics, old lace and memorabilia give it Victorian ambiance.

The two-story glass wall at the back and individual dining nooks and crannies on different levels present ever-changing views of the bayou.

The most romantic spot is on the second level — table P4, a table for two overlooking the bayou through a lace-curtained window.

Private dining rooms have recently been redone with an equestrian theme featuring old English hunting prints.

Antique decoys, tackle and other fishing gear, including five antique outboard motors dating to the '20s, are part of the decor in the dining room. They are from the family collection of owner Donnette Hansen, niece of the original owner, Max Yarbrough.

Hansen has revised the menus to emphasize fresh regional foods that combine traditional and contemporary tastes. Specialties include wild game, Gulf seafood, grilled dishes, and creative sauces using regional ingredients such as fruit, peppers and other fresh vegetables.

Star Attractions

★ Park-like grounds provide a romantic setting for engagements, weddings and anniversaries, especially dinner for two in the Gazebo with a violinist providing music.

★ Party atmosphere — popular for birthdays, anniversaries and other special occasions such as dinner before the prom.

★ Specialties such as Pepper Crusted Filet, a center cut of Certified Angus Beef tenderloin rolled in cracked black pepper; Orvis Salmon, fresh Norwegian salmon topped with lump crabmeat; Lobster Southwest, and regional wild game dishes.

★ Lighter fare including poached fish, grilled chicken, salads, steamed vegetables and avocado salad.

★ Sunday brunch, which also features lighter fare — champagne specials and Mimosas, seafood, pasta, specialty waffles and egg dishes including venison and quail with eggs.

★ Varied wine list that includes American wines, imports and 33 champagnes and sparkling wines.

★ Four private dining rooms including the Wine Room, which seats six; the Hunt Room with fireplace and terrace that seats up to 50; the Tack Room, which seats 12, and the Orvis room, which seats 14.

★ Party and wedding planning — For weddings, Rainbow Lodge will handle everything from invitations, flowers, photographers and music to reception food.

The top layer of your wedding cake can be frozen and held for your first anniversary dinner at the Lodge.

★ Texas Grilling Sauce and Sandia Pepper Jelly Sauce, as featured on the menu, are bottled on the site. Lots of diners are purchasing them for home use or as edible souvenirs.

Medallions of Venison with Cranberry Jalapeno Coulis

Coulis (COO-LEE) is a puree of ingredients used as a sauce.

- **12 (2-ounce) venison tenderloin medallions**
- **2 medium jalapenos, stemmed, seeded and minced**
- **1 (16-ounce) can whole berry cranberry sauce**
- **⅔ cup dry white wine**
- **1 bunch fresh mint (leaves only), minced**

Puree jalapenos in food processor or blender. Add cranberry sauce, wine and mint; process until pureed. Transfer mixture to a heavy pot and simmer over medium heat until sauce will coat the back of a wooden spoon. Keep warm in top of a double boiler over simmering water.

Place venison medallions on hot grill and cook to desired doneness (medium recommended).

Spread warm coulis on about half of each plate. Fan three venison medallions on the sauce. Dribble a little sauce over center medallion and garnish with fresh mint. Good served with roasted potatoes and steamed fresh asparagus.

Serves 4.

🍎 Venison is an extremely low-fat meat. Served with this low-fat sauce, only 9 percent of calories come from fat. Portion recipe for six to limit meat portions to 4 ounces.

Chicken Breast Santa Fe

½   pound bulk chorizo sausage, cooked, drained and cooled to refrigerator temperature

⅓   pound Monterey Jack cheese, grated

½   bunch cilantro (leaves only), minced

4   (4-ounce) boneless, skinless chicken breast halves

1   medium lime

⅛   cup olive oil
    Seasoned flour for dredging

Mix cooled chorizo, cheese and cilantro well. Place chicken breasts between wax paper sheets and pound to a uniform ¼- to ½-inch thick with mallet. Divide the chorizo mix evenly among chicken breasts and stuff them by folding each in half; press edges together or flatten edges with a meat mallet.

Dredge chicken in seasoned flour. Heat oil in saute pan and add the chicken breasts. Squeeze the juice of half the lime over chicken, turn and repeat with remaining lime half. Cook until light golden brown.

Remove chicken to a plate and top with your favorite salsa that has been warmed. Garnish with lime cartwheels and fresh cilantro sprigs. Good accompaniments are Spanish rice and mixed vegetables.

Serves 4.

🍎 Eliminate sausage; use 1 teaspoon olive oil; cut cheese to ¼ pound.

Swordfish San Angelo

    Pineapple Mint Relish (recipe follows)

4   (6-ounce) swordfish steaks

1   cup pineapple juice

Prepare relish and refrigerate at least 4 hours.

Brush swordfish steaks with light oil and place swordfish steaks on a very hot char-grill (2 inches above fire) about 4 minutes, basting with pineapple juice as it cooks. Turn and cook until done, continuing to baste with juice. Transfer steaks to plates and top each liberally with the relish. Accompany with wild rice pilaf or pecan rice and grilled zucchini.

Serves 4.

Good low-fat recipe.

Pineapple Mint Relish

2   large vine ripe tomatoes, cored, seeded and chopped

1   small red onion, cut in ¼-inch dice

1   each: small yellow and green bell peppers, cut in ¼-inch dice

1   medium jalapeno, seeded, stemmed and minced

⅓   fresh pineapple, peeled, cored and cut in ¼-inch dice

1   bunch fresh mint (leaves only), minced

🍎 Combine tomatoes, onion, bell peppers, jalapeno, pineapple and mint leaves in a glass or ceramic (non-metal) bowl. Toss until thoroughly mixed, cover and refrigerate at least 4 hours.

Artichoke Fritters

- 6 artichoke bottoms
- 4 artichoke hearts
- 1 cup water
  Juice of 1 medium lemon
- 4 tablespoons all-purpose flour
- 8 tablespoons seasoned bread crumbs
- ½ teaspoon kosher salt
- 1 teaspoon baking powder
- 2 medium size yellow onions, cut in ¼-inch dice
- 1 tablespoon unsalted butter
- ¼ pound grated Fontina cheese
- 2 large eggs
  Buttermilk and additional bread crumbs for coating
  Peanut oil for deep frying
  Curried Yogurt Sauce (recipe follows)

Heat water to boiling, add lemon juice, artichoke bottoms and hearts; boil 3 minutes. Drain in colander 5 minutes.

Sift flour, bread crumbs, salt and baking powder. Saute onion in butter until soft. Puree artichoke hearts and bottoms until smooth in blender or food processor.

Combine puree, flour mixture, fontina, eggs and sauteed onion in mixing bowl with a paddle and mix on low speed until mixture is thoroughly blended.

Pour buttermilk and bread crumbs in separate flat pans. Using 2 spoons, drop portions of the fritter mixture into the buttermilk and roll until coated. Lift by the spoonful and roll in bread crumbs, coating completely.

Heat peanut oil to 350 degrees in a deep fryer and drop fritters in a few at a time. Cook until deep golden brown. Remove and drain on paper towels. Serve immediately accompanied by Curried Yogurt Sauce.

Curried Yogurt Sauce

- 1 cup plain non-fat or low-fat yogurt
- 2 tablespoons honey
- 1 tablespoon curry powder

Mix yogurt, honey and curry powder and refrigerate covered at least 1 hour for flavors to blend.

🍎 Healthy, low-fat sauce that would be good with steamed or boiled artichokes or other vegetables.

Rainbow Lodge
No. 1 Birdsall
Houston, Texas 77007
861-8666

Taste of Texas

Taste of Texas lives up to its name with a menu of customer-proven favorites starting with superlative beef.

Owner Edd C. Hendee inaugurated the Certified Angus Beef program because he thinks it is the finest beef possible, from steaks to prime rib.

The restaurant has the casual, homey feeling of a Texas ranch house — weathered brick, beamed ceilings, skylights, rustic stone fireplaces with wild game trophies and a stuffed armadillo, wood and brass accents, ceiling fans and hanging ivy and other plants.

Hendee's wife Nina did the decorative stained glass plaques and found the huge quilt used as a wall hanging in one dining room.

In addition to beef, the menu features shrimp, grilled chicken, burgers, soup, gumbo, baked potatoes and fresh vegetable side dishes. Several featured dishes are adapted from recipes from Hendee's or employees' families — such as Ma Maw's Apple Butter and home-baked breads.

With home-style foods and service, Hendee has tried to recreate the feeling of an old-time family restaurant. The whole family is involved in the restaurant's operation.

Community involvement is important at Taste of Texas. Hendee is a member of the Angus Breeder's Association and is a supporter of the Houston Livestock Show & Rodeo and local Future Farmers of America.

Taste of Texas conducts field trips for local area fourth-grade students that include a brief description of the restaurant, tour of the kitchen and a carriage ride.

Taste of Texas will open a new location in January, 1991, down the sreet on the Katy Freeway. It will seat 300. Enjoy wildflowers, a water well and numerous Texas artifacts on 3½ acres.

Star Attractions

★ Certified Angus Beef; steaks are guaranteed to be excellent or they are free. A framed certificate of deposit for $1,000 hangs on one wall; Hendee says he will give it to anyone who finds a better steak of comparable quality and price.

★ Steaks sold by the ounce. "Butchershop" located in the middle of the restaurant where guests can select their own steaks from a butcher's display case and have them cut as thick as they like. Current record is a 101-ounce rib eye selected September 10, 1989, by Trey Hooper, a defensive tackle for the University of Houston.

Hendee recommends a 12-ounce minimum for best flavor. There is no charge for splitting the steak among two or three people. Steaks are served sizzling with butter or lemon pepper seasoning.

All steaks are served as a complete meal with salad bar, cheese block, homemade bread and choice of one side order.

★ Sandwiches such as the Angus Steak Sandwich, a charbroiled slice of Angus rib eye on toasted homemade bread; a Prime Rib Dipper, thin-sliced prime rib on a french loaf with au jus, and the Amarillo Slim burger, choice half-pound beef patty charbroiled and covered with Cheddar cheese.

★ Spacious restaurant that can accommodate large groups; seats 186.

★ Wine list featuring more than 75 selections; particularly strong in California wines. Premium wines by the glass.

★ Specialties including tortilla soup, seafood gumbo, sauteed sweet red onions, baked potatoes and fried okra.

★ Coffee made from Colombian beans freshly ground on the premises. Complimentary Cinnamon Coffee served after the meal.

★ Drink specialties including Texas Style Margarita, Grand Gold Margarita, cinnamon ice cream-amaretto dessert drinks and Frozen Pina Colada.

★ Two large television screens in the club for satellite reception of sports events. Special parties for play-off games. Taste of Texas was the first restaurant to sign a TV satellite agreement to show the Houston Rockets professional basketball games.

★ Newsletter sent periodically to about 9,000 customers on the mailing list. It includes news about restaurant events, new menu items and recipes.

★ Personal response to many diners who fill out comment cards.

★ The Ambassador Pass, a gift certificate for a free meal. Included in the newsletter twice a year and occasionally sent to customers in response to their remarks on comment cards.

Texas Caviar

This is very popular as a cold salad or accompaniment for any Texas-style meal.

1 (15-ounce) can black-eyed peas
1 medium tomato, chopped
3 to 4 green onions, chopped
1 teaspoon fresh minced garlic
½ green bell pepper, finely chopped
¼ cup chopped cilantro
½ cup mild picante sauce
Salt and pepper to taste

Mix peas, tomato, green onion, garlic, bell pepper, cilantro, picante sauce and salt and pepper. Mix well and chill 24 hours in refrigerator before serving.

Serves 8.

High in soluble fiber and low in fat; good choice.

Pasta and Shrimp Salad

The most popular selection on the salad bar at Taste of Texas.

6 ounces dry vermicelli, cooked according to package directions until just tender
6 green onions, thinly chopped
4 teaspoons Pickapeppa sauce (see Note)
1 pound cooked bay shrimp
3 hard-cooked eggs, chopped (optional)
1 cup light mayonnaise
Salt and pepper to taste

Drain cooked vermicelli, rinse with cool water and set aside to cool. Toss lightly with green onion. Add Pickapeppa sauce, shrimp, eggs, mayonnaise, salt and pepper. Toss again lightly. Refrigerate 24 hours before serving.

Serves 4.

Note: Pickapeppa is a Jamaican meat sauce and condiment.

Omit eggs; use ½ cup light mayonnaise; omit salt.

Roast Prime Rib

1 **(4- to 6-pound) Certified Angus Lip-on rib (bone-in rib is fine, but adjust time—cook slower and longer)**
¼ **cup each: kosher and seasoned salt**
2 **tablespoons granulated garlic (not garlic salt)**
½ **cup coarsely ground black pepper**
1 **cup sour cream**
¼ **to ⅓ cup prepared fresh horseradish**

For Seasoning Rub: Mix salts, granulated garlic and pepper. Season outside of meat on all sides putting slightly more on fat. Seasoning 12 hours ahead is recommended.

For Horseradish Sauce: Mix sour cream and horseradish to taste.

Heat oven to 250 degrees. Place roast in deep pan and cover with tent of aluminum foil. Roast slowly 2 to 3 hours until internal temperature reaches 110 degrees on a meat thermometer. Immediately reduce heat to 160 degrees and slow-cook until internal temperature is 135 degrees.

Remove foil tent and broil a few minutes to brown outside of roast. Remove from oven and let stand 10 to 20 minutes. Check doneness with a probe thermometer:

    125-130 degrees – Rare to Medium Rare
    125-140 degrees – Medium Rare to Medium
    145-150 degrees – Medium Well
    155 degrees up – Well Done

Slice and present on a warm plate with horseradish sauce on the side. A 4- to 5-pound roast serves 4 to 5 (10-ounce) finished weight portions.

Caution: The secret to a tender, juicy roast is a controlled slow cooking. Be familiar with your oven and adjust temperature and time if necessary for accuracy. At Taste of Texas, the 12- to 14-pound prime ribs are cooked 8 to 10 hours for tenderness. Don't rush the roast.

South Texas Tenderloin

4 (6-ounce) portions Certified Angus Beef tenderloin
    Lemon pepper seasoning and coarse-ground black pepper
¼ cup butter
1 red onion, thinly sliced
1 pound grated Monterey Jack cheese
2 green onions, finely chopped
    Chives and 1 lime, quartered, for garnish

Season tenderloin with lemon pepper and black pepper to taste. Char-grill to desired doneness. Melt butter in a skillet and simmer red onion until tender.

Slice meat and arrange on a heatproof plate. Top with simmered onions and cover with grated Jack cheese. Broil 3 to 4 minutes until cheese melts. Garnish top with chives and serve with lime wedges on the side. Serve immediately. Good with seasoned rice.

Serves 4.

🍎 Omit butter; use 1 ounce of low-fat cheese per serving.

Taste of Texas Pecan Pie

2 sticks butter, melted
1 cup dark corn syrup
¾ cup sugar
3 eggs, beaten
1 teaspoon vanilla
    Dash of salt
1¼ cups lightly toasted pecan halves
1 unbaked (9-inch) pie shell

Combine melted butter, corn syrup and sugar in a saucepan over low heat. Stir constantly until sugar dissolves. Cool slightly. Add beaten eggs, vanilla and salt; mix well. Stir in pecan halves and pour into pie shell.

Bake at 325 degrees 50 to 55 minutes or until knife inserted in the center comes out clean. Cool until firm before slicing. Serve with Blue Bell vanilla ice cream.

Taste of Texas
90 Town & Country Village on Memorial
Houston, Texas 77024
932-6901

Cooks
& Caterers

Adam's Mark

The Adam's Mark combines the facilities of a first-class hotel and first-class food service. In less than 10 years the hotel has established a reputation for adventurous cuisine in its five restaurants as well as catered events and conventions.

The hotel can cater anything from a wedding rehearsal dinner for 20 to a gala black tie reception for 1,100 in the Grand Ballroom. High school proms and reunions are welcomed.

One of the hotel's biggest attractions is American Western Cuisine, the signature style of executive chef Neil Doherty, one of the region's most talented young chefs.

The Adam's Mark showcase restaurant is The Marker, where the decor is a tasteful mix of Texas ranch and French country house with stucco walls, wood-beamed ceilings, stone fireplace and restful Southwestern desert colors.

The Adam's Mark Catering Department can assist hosts with menus, wine and beverage selections, special diet requests, food presentations/displays, music and entertainment, security, decorations, parking and arrangements for paid checkroom.

Breakfast specials range from sliced fresh fruit, baked apples and fruit yogurt with granola topping to Eggs Benedict or a hearty country breakfast of chicken fried steak with country gravy, biscuits and scrambled eggs.

Luncheons choices vary from fresh fruit plates, veal scallopini or roast pork loin with cider sauerkraut and hot German potato salad to Oriental or Texas barbecue buffets.

The catering dinner menu includes everything from lobster bisque, pecan-smoked veal chop and sauteed chicken breast with champagne mustard sauce to luxurious desserts such as Bailey's Irish Cream Bavarian, Strawberries Romanoff or Texas Chocolate Pecan Pie.

Party menus suit a wide variety of budgets — from a taco bar with spicy chicken or beef and all the fixings to a sophisticated layout of crabmeat on cucumbers, goose liver pate with truffles, American sturgeon caviar and escargot in new potatoes.

Star Attractions

★ American Western-style cuisine features fresh regional ingredients, organically grown vegetables, premium "natural" B3R Texas beef produced without growth hormones or additives, free-range chicken, wild game and fresh-baked breads and pastries.

★ Chef's specialties include meats smoked on the premises, Game Pate with Kiwi Lime Marmalade, Jack Daniels Cured Gravlax, Blacktip Shark Cakes with Mango Chile Yogurt Sauce, Five Onion Soup, Smoked Duckling Breast with Lemon Grass Fusilli and Saki Vinaigrette, Grilled Sirloin with Candied Ancho Chile Butter and Tobacco Onions, Texas T-Bone with Jack Daniels Peppercorn Sauce and Texas Taco, a chocolate waffle taco filled with fresh fruit, cream and pureed berries.

★ Can adapt dishes to meet special diet requirements on request; offer low-cholesterol sauces, pastas prepared without egg yolks, low-fat preparation techniques.

★ Hotel conveniently located in west Houston; 10-story atrium lobby; Houston's largest indoor-outdoor heated swimming pool; health club with jacuzzi and saunas.

★ Live entertainment in Quincy's, a high-energy night club with dancing and casual fare, and Pierre's Lounge with dancing in a romantic atmosphere.

★ Meeting and convention facilities — all on one level — include 31,000 square feet of public space; complimentary surface parking with 1,000-car capacity.

★ Extensive selection of wines, drinks and non-alcoholic drinks including flavored coffees and teas. Excellent wine list with emphasis on California and Texas wines; many wines served by the glass.

★ Lavish Sunday brunch and holiday buffets in The Marker.

★ Vintner Dinners with menus keyed to the wines of the world's greatest wine makers. Recognition by wine and food societies, especially for hosting the Houston Charity Wine Auction benefiting the Covenant House.

★ Grand Ballroom capable of dinners for as many as 800 and receptions for as many as 1,000.

★ Wedding facilities including honeymoon suite and limousine services.

★ Exhibition Center with 14,800 square feet and capacity of 100 booths; separate outside entrance.

★ Two boardrooms with large conference tables, credenzas and plush leather chairs.

★ Catering menus with an extensive selection of items; theme buffets for all kinds of parties from ethnic to history period parties with special foods, flowers, decorations, entertainment, audio-visual equipment.

★ Contributes to the Food Loop program of the End Hunger Network.

Five Onion Soup with Smoked Provolone

2	large yellow onions
1	red onion
3	shallots
2	scallions
1	small leek (white part only)
2	tablespoons olive oil
1	bay leaf
1	teaspoon each: fresh rosemary and thyme
1	teaspoon cracked black peppercorns
1	tablespoon chopped fresh garlic
1	tablespoon chopped fresh parsley
½	cup flour
1	cup Chablis wine
1	quart beef stock or canned beef broth
4	colossal white onions (5 or 6 inches in diameter)
	Toasted croutons
8	slices smoked Provolone cheese

Finely slice onions, shallots, scallions and leek. Saute in oil with bay leaf, rosemary and thyme, peppercorns, garlic and parsley until translucent.

Stir in flour lightly. Cook, stirring, until browned like a roux; add wine and simmer over medium heat 5 minutes. Add beef stock and simmer 15 to 20 minutes. Correct seasoning.

Hollow out colossal onions, but do not pierce bottoms.

Just before serving, blanch onion "bowls" in hot or boiling salted water just long enough for them to retain heat.

To serve: Ladle soup into onions and float toasted croutons on top. Cover each onion with 2 slices smoked provolone and melt under broiler.

Serves 4.

🍎 Use 1 tablespoon olive oil; substitute 2 ounces part-skim mozzarella for cheese.

Smoked Texas Longhorn Tenderloin

1   **whole beef tenderloin, smoked**
      Black pepper
¼   **cup olive oil**
      Adobo or other favorite seasoning

Soak about 1 cup pecan chips in water overnight.

Trim beef, removing all fat and tendons. To equalize thickness, fold thinner end under or cut off about 5 or 6 inches of the tail end and use for another purpose such as stroganoff or kabobs.

Sprinkle pepper on tenderloin and rub olive oil over surface. Place in smoker to one side of charcoal fire (make a nest of 6 to 8 pieces charcoal and fill with pecan chips). Smoke, covered, at low temperature 35 to 45 minutes.

Transfer meat to shallow pan and finish to desired doneness in preheated 350-degree oven until meat is done — 125 to 130 degrees internal temperature for medium rare; 120 for rare.

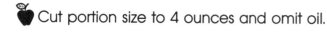 Cut portion size to 4 ounces and omit oil.

Candied Ancho Chile Butter
  1   **cup diced ancho chilies (dried poblanos)**
  ½   **cup each: sugar and water**
  1   **pound butter, cut in cubes**
      Salt and pepper to taste

Boil sugar and water with ancho chilies until almost caramelized. Cool. Pour chilies and liquid into food processor and add butter, a little at a time. Butter should not melt.

Pour into a shallow sheet pan and chill until firm. Cut pieces with a star cookie cutter or other shape. To serve, fan 4 or 5 thin pieces of tenderloin on a plate. Place butter on top. Garnish plate with a small bouquet of fresh herbs or with black bean or smoked corn relish.

Serves 6.

Dressed to Grill.

Lone Star Polenta

2 **cups milk**
¾ **cup yellow cornmeal**
Pinch of mace
Salt and pepper to taste
2 **egg yolks, beaten**
2 **ounces (4 tablespoons) butter**

Bring milk to a boil in a 1- or 1½-quart saucepan. Sprinkle in cornmeal. Simmer 5 minutes over low heat, whisking constantly, until thick. Season with mace, salt and pepper. Remove from heat.

Whisk in egg yolks and butter; stir until butter melts. Pour mixture into a shallow, greased sheet pan with ¼-inch sides. Smooth evenly. Let cool at room temperature until set. Cover with plastic wrap and refrigerate until cold. Cut into longhorn, stars or other shapes with cookie cutter.

Before serving, grill until hot on an oiled grill rack, "skin side" down.

Serves 6.

Substitute skim milk for whole; use 2 table-spoons soft margarine instead of 4 tablespoons butter; use ¼ cup egg substitute instead of 2 egg yolks.

Hill Country Peach Snow with Texas Dewberries

1 pound poached fresh peaches, reserve syrup (see Note)
2½ cups water
1 cup sugar
  Dash of vanilla
¼ cup whipping cream
⅓ cup raspberry vinegar
⅓ cup honey
  Dewberries or black berries for garnish

Note: To poach peaches: peel, seed and cut peaches into wedges; bring water and sugar to a boil; add vanilla; add peaches and poach a few minutes, just until a toothpick can be inserted into the peach without resistance.

Place poached peaches and half the syrup in an electric blender or food processor. With motor running, gradually add cream and remaining syrup. Freeze in ice cream machine according to manufacturer's directions. Or pour into a pan and freeze in refrigerator until firm, stirring every 30 minutes.

For sauce, blend raspberry vinegar and honey.

To serve: Spoon sauce into glass, add one scoop of peach ice and surround with 6 or 8 dewberries. Margarita or martini glasses make attractive serving dishes.

Makes about 1 quart.

Low-fat dessert, but high in sugar.

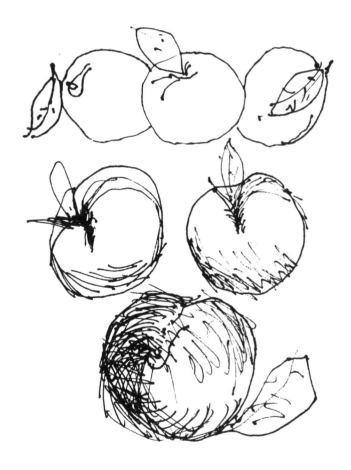

Jalapeno Ice Cream

This has a unique flavor— the cold creamy texture offsets the heat of the jalapenos.

- 2 **eggs plus 2 egg yolks**
- 6 **tablespoons sugar**
- 1¾ **cups milk**
- 1 **teaspoon vanilla extract**
- 1 **cup heavy (whipping) cream**
- 4 **ounces fresh jalapenos, seeded and finely diced**
- ½ **cup each: sugar and water**

Beat eggs and yolks with sugar until smooth and thick. Heat the milk to scalding (until bubbles form at edges). Carefully pour into egg, whisking constantly.

Strain mixture into the top of a double boiler placed over simmering water. Stir over low heat until thickened.

Bring sugar and water to a boil in a saucepan; let simmer a few minutes over high heat until syrupy, add jalapenos and boil until candied, about 4 to 5 minutes. Strain and discard excess liquid.

Add vanilla and candied jalapeno to ice cream mixture. Fold in lightly whipped cream, pour into ice cream machine and freeze according to manufacturer's directions or freeze in a tray in refrigerator freezer.

Beat every 30 minutes for 2 hours, or until set.

Timesaver: Substitute mild-flavored commercial vanilla ice cream for homemade. Let it soften somewhat and stir in candied jalapeno mixture along with syrupy liquid; refreeze.

Makes 1 quart.

Southern Comfort Pecan Pie

- ½ **stick (4 tablespoons) butter**
- ½ **cup granulated sugar**
- ½ **pound (8 ounces) brown sugar**
- 5 **eggs**
- ⅔ **cup dark corn syrup**
- 1 **teaspoon vanilla extract**
- 2 **ounces Southern Comfort**
- 1 **(9⅝-inch) unbaked pie shell**
- 8 **ounces pecan pieces**

Combine butter, white and brown sugar in a skillet and cook until butter is melted. Whip to blend; let cool.

In a bowl, beat eggs lightly; whip into butter-sugar mixture with corn syrup, vanilla and Southern Comfort. Fit pastry into pie pan.

Place pecan pieces in bottom of pie shell and fill to within ½ inch of top with filling mixture. Bake at 375 degrees until a knife inserted in center comes out clean, about 40 to 45 minutes.

If pie shell begins to brown too much, cover edges with a strip of foil.

adam's mark®
houston

Adam's Mark
2900 Briarpark at Westheimer
Houston, Texas 77042
978-7400

Backstreet Cafe

Backstreet Cafe and Prego, both owned by Tracy Vaught and her uncle Jack Blalock, are taking on new character inspired by a talented presence in the kitchen, chef John Watt.

Vaught, a geophysicist at Conoco who "dropped out" when the oil decline hit Houston in the early '80s, opened the restaurant in 1984 in an old two-story house on a short backstreet offshoot of South Shepherd.

Although Backstreet retains its casual, pleasant bistro ambiance, it is now a showcase for more contemporary American regional food such as sauteed trout in spicy blue corn-meal jacket with cilantro lime butter; prime New York strip with jalapeno Bearnaise and a grilled fresh tuna version of the classic French Salade Nicoise.

Star Attractions

★ Casual sidewalk cafe atmosphere. Open-air dining at umbrella tables under a showy camphor tree in the midst of a flower-decked New Orleans-style fountain patio or on a terrace deck. Seats 90 inside, 80 outside.

★ Convenient to downtown, Heights, Montrose and River Oaks areas.

★ Private party rooms. Patio and private upstairs dining room with adjoining terrace offer pleasant settings for weddings, receptions, luncheons and parties.

★ New American Bistro cuisine — the menu has evolved from simple soups and sandwiches to inspired cooking by young chef John Watt. Fresh, Texas-grown ingredients used whenever possible.

★ Backstreet specialties: Salade Nicoise with fresh grilled tuna; grilled shrimp in ginger-soy-sesame sauce with whole-wheat linguini; Roasted Hickory Smoked Tomato Sauce achieved by cold smoking tomatoes (see recipe); grilled chicken breast over mixed greens with toasted pecans, Texas Ruby Red grapefruit, avocado and Maytag blue cheese tossed with a champagne vinaigrette; honey-sesame back baby ribs with grilled green onions; spicy crab balls with hollandaise and roasted red pepper sauce; chicken quesadillas.

★ Late hours (until 2 a.m. on Fridays and Saturdays).

★ Sunday brunch.

★ Brown bag lunches.

★ Extensive list of wines by the glass.

Roast Corn and Shrimp Salad

½ cup cooked black beans
½ cup roasted corn
¼ cup each: roasted yellow and red bell peppers (see Peppers in Special Helps section)
4 to 6 arugula leaves
4 jumbo shrimp, boiled
3 small pieces feta cheese (about 1 ounce)
1 red onion, sliced and separated into rings
Spa Dressing (recipe follows)

All ingredients should be chilled. Arrange salad on an oval plate in this order: arugula on right side; row of black beans; row of corn; row of peppers; shrimp on upper left side. Sprinkle feta cheese and red onion rings over salad. Top with dressing or serve dressing on the side.

Spa Dressing

2 tablespoons reduced vegetable stock by half or vegetable bouillon
1 tablespoon brown rice vinegar
1 tablespoon fresh lime juice
Pinch of sea salt

Whisk stock, vinegar, lime juice and salt together.

This recipe has only 18 percent fat calories. Enjoy!

Roast Chicken Breast with Chipotle and Sweet Marsala Sauce

1 (7-ounce) boneless, skinless chicken breast
Olive oil, garlic and fresh rosemary
4 ounces strong veal stock or chicken bouillon
4 ounces sweet Marsala wine
½ to 1 tablespoon canned chipotle with adobo sauce, pureed
½ tablespoon butter
Cilantro sprigs for garnish

Marinate chicken breast in a little olive oil, chopped garlic and fresh rosemary at least 4 hours, covered, in the refrigerator. Roast or grill to your liking.

Meanwhile, combine stock, Marsala and chipotle sauce and simmer until reduced to a syrupy stage. Remove from heat and whisk in cold butter to finish sauce and give it a nice sheen. Serve over chicken. Garnish with cilantro.

Serves 1.

Use 1 teaspoon olive oil to marinate chicken. The Sweet Marsala Sauce is low in fat and sodium, so, enjoy.

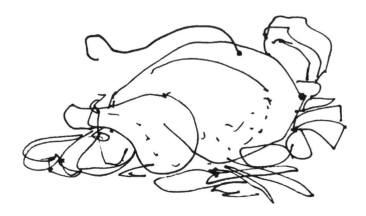

Prego

Prego also retains its casual neighborhood restaurant character, but chef John Watt gives it modern Italian flair; his new menus also include several healthful Spa Cuisine specialties.

The restaurant attracts a mixed crowd of varying ages from West University Place, Rice University, the Texas Medical Center and surrounding neighborhoods as well as the inner city.

The long, narrow resturant is visually defined by the pressed tin ceiling and beautifully carved bar opposite a wall of banquettes.

Star Attractions

★ Small, Italian trattoria-style neighborhood restaurant seats 65.

★ Small wine room for private parties.

★ Lighter, creative contemporary Italian fare based on fresh regional ingredients, pasta, Hickory Smoked Roasted Tomato Sauce, balsamic vinegar, Italian herbs.

★ Specialties: South of the Border Fettuccine with grilled chicken, jalapeno pasta, black beans and cilantro; stone oven pizzas; grilled scallops over arugula with diced mangos, tomatoes, avocado, black beans and red onion in brown rice vinegar and lime juice; paillards of chicken marinated in balsamic vinegar, garlic and rosemary.

★ Extensive list of wines by the glass.

Crawfish Tails and Shiitake Mushrooms Over Angel Hair Pasta in Garlic Cream

4 ounces crawfish tails
1 tablespoon chopped garlic
Olive oil
1 cup heavy (whipping) cream or half-and-half
4 ounces freshly grated Parmesan cheese
Salt and white pepper to taste
2 to 3 ounces shiitake mushrooms
Cracked black pepper
1 tablespoon chopped green onion
4 ounces angel hair pasta, cooked al dente
½ tablespoon (1½ teaspoons) dry white wine
Fresh mint and dried roast red pepper flakes for garnish

Saute garlic in ½ teaspoon oil over low temperature until lightly browned. Add cream and simmer until it comes to a light boil. Whisk in Parmesan, salt and white pepper to taste. Let cook until reduced to sauce consistency.

Saute crawfish tails in another pan in 1 tablespoon olive oil with shiitake mushrooms and green onion; sprinkle with cracked black pepper. Deglaze with wine (stir and scrape bits from bottom). Toss pasta with cream sauce. Top with crawfish mixture. Garnish with fresh mint and pepper flakes. Grate a little Parmesan over the top.

Serves 1 or 2 as a side dish.

Substitute evaporated skim milk for cream. Crawfish are high in cholesterol. Cut Parmesan to 2 ounces; total olive oil, 1 teaspoon.

Hickory Smoked Tomato Sauce

This sauce has a distinctive smoky flavor that compliments everything from pasta to nachos. It's labor intensive, but deliciously different.

- 10 pounds Roma tomatoes, cut off stem ends
- 2 medium-size white onions, peeled and trimmed on both sides
  Small pan of hickory chips that have soaked in water at least 2 hours
- 1 cup diced garlic
- 2 cups fresh basil
- ¼ to ½ cup olive oil
- 2 cups white wine
- 1 quart strong chicken stock
- ½ pound butter
  Salt and black pepper

Place tomatoes, cut stem side down, and onions in a single layer on ovenproof plate on rack in cold oven. Drain hickory chips and heat over high heat, covered, until they begin to smoke (this can get messy and ruin the pan; it's best to use the same pan for smoking every time). Remove cover and transfer pan to oven on rack below tomatoes; close door tightly. Tomatoes will be properly smoked when they sweat through the skin, about 10 minutes. Chop tomatoes and onions.

Saute garlic and basil in olive oil; add chopped onion and wine and let reduce slightly, 2 or 3 minutes. Turn into large stock pot.

Add chicken stock and butter; salt and pepper to taste. Let cook until reduced by half. Makes about 2 gallons. Cool to room temperature, and store in refrigerator.

Use as a pasta or pizza sauce, with crab claws sauteed with basil and roast pepper flakes, or use as a topping for bruschetta (an Italian bread appetizer). Can also be used on nachos with queso blanco or mozzarella cheese, black beans, jalapenos and smoked, cooked shrimp if desired.

Saute garlic, onion and basil in wine and eliminate butter and olive oil.

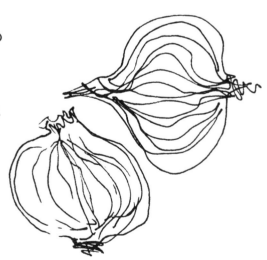

Catering Star Attractions

★ Off-site catering for as many as 2,000.

★ Custom menus for weddings, receptions, graduation parties, business meetings, bar and bas mitzvahs, kosher events (with advance notice of a week), ethnic dinner parties (Russian, French, Italian, tapas appetizers, Southwestern, Creole or Tex-Mex).

★ Wine tastings and vintner dinners.

Reception for 200

Exotic Fruit and Cheese Display

Crudites with Roasted Eggplant Sauce

Boiled Gulf Shrimp and Fresh Gulf Oysters with Fresh Herb Remoulade and Cocktail Sauce

Country Pate with Homemade Croutons

Chicken Mousse with Pistachios

Asparagus Wrapped with Tasso Served with Cold Herb Mayonnaise

Roasted New Potatoes Stuffed with Sour Cream and Caviar

Roast Tenderloin of Beef with Cognac au Jus

Catering menus from Backstreet and Prego

Rehearsal Dinner for 50

Tri Pepper Fresh Gravlax of Salmon with Fresh Herbs,

Dark Rye Toast and Dill Chutney

Cucumber Soup with Crawfish Cream

Mixed Baby Lettuces with Goat Cheese and Grilled Shiitakes

Veal Chop with Marsala Sauce and Porcini Mushrooms

Layers of Toasted Almond Meringue and Liqueur-Soaked Genoise with Mango Cream and Strawberries

Light Cocktail Reception

Fresh Cured Salmon Springrolls

Pasta Station with Fusilli with Roasted Tomato Sauce and Grilled Shrimp

Grilled Brochettes of Tenderloin of Beef and Vegetables with Teriyaki Sauce

Imported Cheese Display

Melon Platter

Backstreet Cafe
1103 S. Shepherd
Houston, Texas 77019
521-2239

Prego
2520 Amherst (Rice University Village)
Houston, Texas 77005
529-2420

Carrabba's

Carrabba's restaurants operate with the lively, happy atmosphere of a family reunion. And well they might. Family tradition is the hallmark of Carrabba's and eight more of Houston's most popular restaurants that spring from the Mandola family tree.

Damian's Cucina Italiana (owned by Damian Mandola), Nino's and Vincent's (owned by Damian's brother Vincent Mandola) and Tony Mandola's (owned by brother Tony Mandola) set the pace. Cousins Johnny Carrabba and Damian Mandola are co-owners of Carrabba's, which has been one of the big success stories in Houston restaurants almost from the day it opened on Kirby Drive in 1986. The second Carrabba's, convenient to the Tanglewood and Memorial areas, opened in 1988.

The food combines family tradition with modern American flair from a home-style version of spaghetti and meatballs to Margherita Pizza baked to perfection in a wood-burning oven. Carrabba's on Kirby has recently built a 30x50-foot kitchen, which will produce food for both the restaurant and expanded catering operation. A covered patio with ceiling fans and eight-table dining room also were added.

Star Attractions

★ Casual, fun atmosphere, but not intimidating for the theater-goer in black tie dress who stops in for a late-night meal.

★ Authentic Italian cooking from a small, but consistent menu — popular pasta dishes such as Penne Mary Raia and Fettuccine with salmon. Variety of fresh-made pizzas baked in a wood-burning oven. Fresh fish cooked on an open grill.

★ Two locations; one convenient to West University Place, the Summit, Texas Medical Center and River Oaks, and the other, to the Tanglewood and Memorial areas.

★ Great people-watching and meeting place; Carrabba's attracts local and national celebrities and an interesting mix of neighborhood regulars.

★ Open kitchen where diners can see food being prepared.

★ Outdoor patio seating.

★ Private dining room that accommodates 15 at Voss Road location.

★ Friendly, hands-on management; Johnny Carrabba is usually around welcoming customers or cooking.

Caponata

2   **pounds eggplant, peeled and cut into ½-inch cubes (about 8 cups) Salt**

½   **cup olive oil**

2   **cups finely chopped celery**

¾   **cup finely chopped onion**

⅓   **cup wine vinegar mixed with 4 teaspoons sugar**

3   **cups drained canned Italian plum or whole tomatoes**

2   **tablespoons tomato paste**

6   **large green olives, pitted, slivered and well rinsed**

2   **tablespoons capers**

4   **flat anchovy fillets, rinsed well and pounded smooth with a mortar and pestle Freshly ground black pepper**

2   **tablespoons pine nuts (pignolia)**

Sprinkle eggplant cubes generously with salt and set them in a colander or large sieve over paper towels to drain for about 30 minutes. Pat cubes dry with fresh paper towels and set aside.

Heat ¼ cup olive oil in heavy 12- to 14-inch skillet. Add celery and cook over moderate heat, stirring frequently, 10 minutes. Stir in onion and cook 8 to 10 minutes or until celery and onion are soft and lightly colored. With a slotted spoon, transfer them to a bowl.

Pour remaining olive oil into skillet and saute eggplant cubes in it over high heat, stirring and turning them constantly about 8 minutes, or until lightly browned. Return celery and onion to skillet and stir in vinegar-sugar mixture, drained tomatoes, tomato paste, olives, capers, anchovies, 2 teaspoons salt and a few grindings of pepper.

Bring to a boil, reduce heat and simmer uncovered, stirring frequently, about 15 minutes. Stir in the pinenuts. Taste the mixture and season with salt and pepper and a little extra vinegar if necessary.

Transfer to a serving bowl, cover and refrigerate until ready to serve. Serve with garlic toast.

Makes 8 cups.

🍎 Use ¼ cup olive oil for sauteing the vegetables. Serve with plain toast, flat bread or lahvash.

Pasta Frittata
(Frittata di Pasta)

1 **pound dried pasta such as penne**
   Coarse-grained salt
2 **ounces (4 tablespoons) sweet butter**
9 **extra-large eggs**
⅓ **cup freshly grated Parmesan cheese**
10 **fresh mint leaves**
6 **or 7 large fresh basil leaves**
5 **sprigs Italian parsley, leaves only,**
   finely chopped
   Freshly ground pepper
1 **scant tablespoon olive oil**

Bring a large pot of cold water to a boil. Add coarse-grained salt to taste, drop in the pasta and cook until it is al dente. Drain and transfer to a large bowl with the butter. Toss very well so butter completely coats cooked pasta. Cover the bowl and let stand about 20 minutes.

Beat the eggs with a fork in a large bowl. Add Parmesan, mint leaves, 3 basil leaves torn into small pieces and chopped parsley. Taste for salt and pepper. Add the cooled pasta and mix thoroughly. Place a 10-inch omelet pan over heat and add the oil.

When oil is hot, add egg mixture and cook frittata until egg is set. Turn frittata onto a plate and slide it back into the pan to cook second side until done. Reverse frittata onto a serving dish. Spread remaining basil leaves over top and serve.

Serves 6.

🍎 Use 6 whole eggs and 6 egg whites; substitute 2 tablespoons soft margarine for butter; spray omelet pan with non-stick cooking spray.

Penne Mary Raia

Named for Mary Raia, Johnny Carrabba's wife.

12	ounces clarified butter (see Special Helps section)
2	tablespoons chopped shallots
18	medium mushrooms, sliced
½	cup prosciutto, thinly sliced and cut in julienne strips
1½	cups heavy (whipping) cream
¾	cup green peas (can use frozen)
1½	pounds dried penne pasta
1½	cups freshly grated Parmesan cheese Salt and pepper

Place butter, shallots, mushrooms and prosciutto in large skillet over medium high heat. Saute 2 to 3 minutes, then add cream and peas. Let simmer to reduce for a minute.

Meanwhile, cook pasta in boiling salted water as directed on package until al dente. Drain pasta; add to skillet and toss. Add Parmesan, salt and pepper and toss again to coat well. Place in bowl and serve immediately.

Serves 6.

Substitute evaporated skim milk for cream; omit salt; use 6 tablespoons soft margarine and ¾ cup Parmesan.

Beefsteak Pizzaiola (Bisteca Pizzaiola)

4   (8-ounce) ribeye or filet mignon steaks
4   tablespoons extra-virgin olive oil
     Salt and freshly ground pepper
3   cups Pizzaiola sauce (recipe follows)
8   tablespoons freshly grated Parmesan
     or Romano
4   ounces shredded Mozzarella

Rub olive oil over steaks. Salt and pepper each. Place on grill and cook to desired doneness. Transfer to platter; top each steak with ¾ cup heated Pizzaiola Sauce. Sprinkle with grated Parmesan, then with Mozzarella. Place under broiler until cheese melts. Serve immediately.

Serves 4.

Pizzaiola Sauce
2   ounces extra-virgin olive oil
1   small yellow onion, sliced medium-thick
     Pinch of red pepper flakes
¼   teaspoon dried oregano
8   ounces canned tomatoes, chopped
     Salt and pepper to taste
1   tablespoon chopped fresh basil
2   to 3 tablespoons coarsely chopped
     garlic
15   pitted Calamata olives

Heat oil in skillet and add onions; saute until soft. Add pepper flakes, oregano, tomatoes, salt, pepper, basil and garlic; simmer about 10 minutes. Add olives; stir. Remove from heat; refrigerate to store.

Makes 1 quart.

🍎 Reduce steak portion to 4 ounces; omit oil before grilling; use 1 tablespoon Parmesan, ½ ounce mozzarella, 4 ounces Pizzaiola sauce; prepare without salt and oil.

Catering Star Attractions

★ Additional dining area that can be screened off for private parties.

★ Will deliver catering orders or provide full-service catering off premises.

★ Buffet menu includes antipasto, pasta, salad, entree, garlic bread and choice of dessert.

★ Antipasti Misto — choice of three Italian appetizers including Caponata (the eggplant relish that is a signature dish of the restaurant) and sweet and sour snapper.

★ Wide variety of pasta specialties including Rigatoni Campagnola with Italian sausage, sweet peppers and goat cheese in marinara sauce to Cappelletti, "Pope's hats" shaped pasta stuffed with chicken, spinach and Parmesan in tomato cream sauce.

★ Several chicken dishes plus quail wrapped in pancetta (Italian bacon) and fresh sage served over grilled polenta with Marsala sauce.

★ Fish specialties including Shrimp and Scallops Sauteed with tomato, garlic and lemon butter sauce served with Penne Alfredo; Norwegian Salmon with cucumber, tomato relish and roasted garlic potatoes and Grilled Swordfish and Shrimp with pineapple, basil and tomato relish served with Italian rice.

★ Make all fresh pastas.

★ Gift certificates.

★ Desserts include a classic Tiramisu (Italian double cream Mascarpone cheese mousse layered between espresso-soaked ladyfingers and dusted with chocolate); Cappuccino Terrine (layered mousse of white, dark and semisweet chocolate); fresh seasonal fruit tarts; an assortment of bakery-fresh cookies — biscotti amaretto, chocolate and sand tarts; Amaretto Cheesecake with strawberries, and Death by Chocolate, layered brownie mousse cake.

Carrabba's
3115 Kirby Dr.
Houston, Texas 77098
522-3131

Carrabba's
1399 S. Voss Road
Houston, Texas 77057
468-0868

Empress of China

Nouvelle Chinese Cuisine is an innovative style of Chinese cooking created by Empress of China owners Scott Chen and Richard Ho to blend ideas, ingredients and traditional cooking techniques of many different cuisines. The food is Chinese; the presentation, French.

However, instead of resorting to the expected and often trite stir-frys, Chen employs cooking techniques that result in lighter, healthier dishes — steaming, poaching, boiling, braising, sauteeing, grilling and broiling — or a combination.

Wok "firing" and broth cooking replace frying. In wok firing, the combination of heating the oil to a very high temperature and using a lighter breading prevents retention of grease. In broth cooking, no fat is used; foods are cooked in broth, then flambeed in spices.

Still, the No. 1 consideration is good taste. Skillful cooking, seasoning and presentation elevate the food to gourmet status, and the restaurant also has received accolades from gourmet societies and corporations that have entertained there.

Likewise, Richard Ho does not feel bound by tradition in matching wines to the dishes, and makes gifted pairings with the Chinese food from an extensive list ranging from French Pouilly Fuisse to California Cabernet. He lists more than 50 fine Bordeaux alone, and is assembling the best collection of Alsatian wines in Houston.

The decor of the 95-seat restaurant also is non-traditional. The contemporary feeling is created by neutral colors punctuated by deep green carpeting and table linens, caneback chairs and planter boxes filled with fresh flowers.

Although the nouvelle dishes are lower in calories, sodium and cholesterol, they are appealing in flavors and ample in portions.

Natural flavors of the ingredients are accentuated, and no monosodium glutamate flavor enhancer is used. Low-sodium soy sauce and Maggi seasoning are often substituted for soy sauce.

Classics are modified to reduce fat; sweet and sour pork, for example, is made with 98 percent fat-free pork.

Chen's family immigrated to Houston from Taiwan in 1981, and he became interested in cooking while working at The Ambassador, a Chinese restaurant owned by his sister-in-law. While working at Uncle Tai's restaurant he learned the classic Hunan-style cooking. Travels have broadened his appreciation of many cuisines.

Richard Ho was born in Hong Kong but grew up in Lubbock, Texas, where he earned bachelor's and master's degrees at Texas Tech University. He also has a master's degree in business administration from the University of Houston.

Ho, his wife Vicky and Chen are the three major stockholders in the restaurant corporation.

Star Attractions

★ Nouvelle Chinese Cuisine, innovative lighter, healthier cooking style that emphasizes good taste and incorporates the best tastes and cooking techniques of many cuisines.

Specialties include Oriental beef or chicken "fajitas" and several dishes with fanciful names — Sand on the Snow (chicken flambeed with black pepper and a wine sauce), the Neptune's Platter (sea scallops, shrimp and crab with black bean sauce) and Romeo and Juliet (scallops in a spicy ginger sauce for two).

New menu items include Veal with Fresh Basil, stir-fried veal strips with fresh basil, other herbs and spices; lamb sliced and sauteed with fresh mint and Texas sweet onions and pasta dishes including seafood angelhair pasta with fresh tomato sauce.

★ Open kitchen policy during operating hours. Guests may visit kitchen on request.

★ Daily specials — both food and wine.

★ Extensive wine list with about 200 selections including 50 fine Bordeaux. Excellent price-to-value ratio; prices challenge those in retail shops. Two or three new wines are featured every week. Currently any wine featured as a weekly special is $12 a bottle.

★ Special attention is paid to freshness of ingredients and combination of herbs, seasonings and sauces that enhance rather than smother. No artificial flavors or preservatives are used. Because each dish is prepared to order, spiciness or ingredient selections can be adjusted to the guest's taste. Foods can be broth cooked instead of fried.

★ Moderately priced Sunday brunch buffet of 15 courses.

★ Gourmet wine dinners and party menus. Six to 10-course special banquet available for groups of more than seven. Monthly gourmet wine and food pairing dinners, usually the last Sunday of the month.

★ Cooking classes including supermarket shopping trip can be arranged.

★ Registered dietitian serves as menu consultant.

★ Delivery within a 10-minute drive of the restaurant.

★ All menu items available for take-out.

Empress Barbecued Spareribs

1	pound small, lean pork ribs
1	teaspoon rice wine
1	teaspoon soy sauce
½	teaspoon salt
2	teaspoons sugar
2	teaspoons hoisin sauce or ketchup
⅛	teaspoon Chinese five-spice powder
3	garlic cloves, finely minced
2	green onions (including tops), finely chopped

Rinse and drain ribs; pat dry. Place ribs in large bowl with combined rice wine, soy sauce, salt, sugar, hoisin, five-spice powder, garlic and green onion; stir to coat well. Marinate at least 1 hour, turning frequently to evenly coat ribs with marinade.

Preheat oven to 450 degrees. Arrange ribs on a baking pan on middle rack of the oven.

Bake 30 minutes, basting occasionally. To test for doneness, prick with a fork; if liquid is clear, ribs are done. Cut into individual pieces and serve.

Serves 2 to 3.

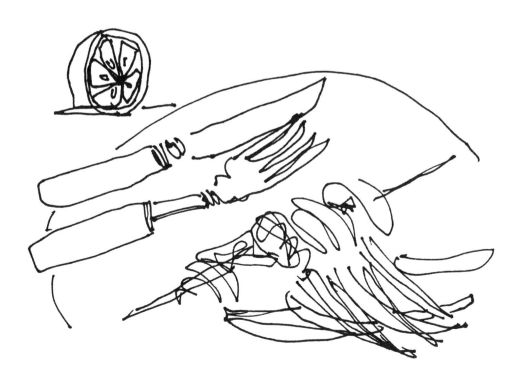

Glazed Prawns with Ganshi Sauce

10 prawns (jumbo shrimp), tails intact
1 tablespoon cornstarch
2 tablespoons water
2 cups peanut oil + 3 teaspoons
1 tablespoon minced onion
1 teaspoon minced fresh ginger
2 teaspoons minced garlic
5 tablespoons tomato sauce
1 teaspoon hot bean sauce (available in Chinese markets)

Seasoning
1 teaspoon wine
½ teaspoon salt
1 teaspoon soy sauce
2 teaspoons sugar
3 tablespoons chicken stock

Remove shells from prawns, rinse lightly and pat dry. Slice halfway through prawns lengthwise through thick part; devein. Dissolve cornstarch in water in a bowl.

Heat wok or pan and add peanut oil. Heat to about 250 degrees. Add prawns and stir-fry 15 seconds. Remove and drain wok.

Clean pan and add 3 teaspoons oil. Stir-fry onion, ginger and garlic a few seconds. Add tomato sauce and hot bean sauce; mix well.

Add seasoning ingredients and prawns; bring to a boil. Reduce heat and simmer until there is almost no juice left. Stir in cornstarch and stir until thickened. Turn onto serving dish.

Serves 2 or more if you have other dishes.

Cook prawns in 2 cups boiling broth; use 1 teaspoon oil for stir-frying meat and seasonings. Use low-sodium soy sauce.

Eggplant with Garlic Sauce

2 eggplants, rinsed and peeled
2 ounces ground pork or beef
1 cup flour
½ teaspoon baking powder
¾ cup water
2 teaspoons cornstarch
5 cups oil
  Seasoning (recipe follows)

Cut off eggplant stems and ends. Slice diagonally ¾-inch thick. For batter, whisk flour and baking powder into water; whisk in cornstarch until smooth. Dip each eggplant slice into batter to coat lightly.

Meanwhile, heat wok, add oil and bring it to a low boil. Deep-fry eggplant slices to golden brown, a few at a time. Remove and drain well. Arrange eggplant on a plate.

Seasoning

1 teaspoon minced green onion
1 teaspoon minced ginger
1 teaspoon minced garlic
1 teaspon hot bean sauce
1 tablespoon chicken stock
1 teaspoon each: soy sauce and vinegar
½ teaspoon ground pepper
2 teaspoons cornstarch
4 teaspoons oil

For sauce: mix seasonings well in a bowl: green onion, ginger, garlic, bean sauce, stock, soy sauce, vinegar and pepper. Dissolve cornstarch in mixture. Heat 4 teaspoons oil in wok. Stir-fry ground meat and seasoning over high heat until done, less than a minute. Pour mixture and sauce over the eggplant patties.

Serves 4 to 6.

Note: Scallops or shrimp may be substituted for meat.

Broth-Cooked Shredded Pork & Scallion

½ **pound pork tenderloin**
2 **teaspoons cornstarch**
4 **teaspoons water**
2 **cups chicken broth**
1 **tablespoon oil**
5 **green onions including tops**

Seasoning
2½ **teaspoons hoisin sauce**
2 **teaspoons wine or sherry**
1 **teaspoon soy sauce**
⅔ **teaspoon sugar**
1 **teaspoon sesame oil**

Shred pork into ⅛-inch strips. Dissolve 1 teaspoon cornstarch in 2 teaspoons water. Marinate pork strips in cornstarch mixture 15 minutes. Cut green onions into 2-inch strips.

Bring broth to a rolling boil. Put meat in a strainer and lower into boiling broth over high heat until cooked, about 2 minutes. Be sure pork strips do not stick together. Remove from pan.

Clean wok or pan, heat and add 1 tablespoon oil. When oil boils, add scallions and stir-fry 10 seconds. Add pork and seasoning: hoisin sauce, wine, soy sauce, sugar and sesame oil. Mix well. Dissolve remaining teaspoon cornstarch in remaining water. Add to mixture in wok and stir until sauce thickens. Remove from heat and serve.

Serves 2 to 4.

🍎 Use 1 teaspoon oil to stir-fry; use low-sodium soy sauce. Serve with plain boiled rice.

Beef a la Scott

1¼	pounds beef tenderloin
1	teaspoon salt
1	teaspoon ground white pepper
3	teaspoons cooking wine or sherry
3	eggs, well mixed
2	teaspoons cornstarch
½	cup plain dry bread crumbs
6	cups oil plus 1 teaspoon oil
½	ounce dried chilies (such as jalapenos)
2	teaspoons chopped green onion
1	teaspoon minced garlic
3	teaspoons sugar
3	teaspoons water

Seasoning

2	teaspoons each: soy sauce and sugar
1	teaspoon vinegar
2	tablespoons beef stock or water
1	teaspoon minced ginger

Cut tenderloin into 2-inch strips. Marinate n salt, pepper, 2 teaspoons wine, beaten eggs and cornstarch. Coat with bread crumbs. Heat wok or pan and add 6 cups oil; heat to 350 degrees. Deep-fry beef strips to golden brown, 5 to 7 minutes, in several batches. Remove and drain wok.

Clean wok and reheat. Add 1 teaspoon oil. Stir-fry dried chilies 15 seconds. Add green onion, garlic, sugar, remaining teaspoon wine and 2 teaspoons cornstarch which have been dissolved in water.

Add cooked beef strips and seasonings: soy sauce, sugar, vinegar, stock and ginger. Mix well and let simmer 5 to 10 seconds. Remove and serve.

Serves 4 to 6.

General tips: serve dishes with plain boiled rice. Use low-sodium soy sauce and omit salt. Ask that dishes be prepared in boiling broth instead of fried.

Catering Star Attractions

★ Can provide formal to informal catering from buffets and luaus to white-glove service for black-tie occasions.

★ Can just deliver food, provide staff to set up and serve buffet-style or provide full staff, including bartenders, for multi-course dinners with full china service.

★ Customized menus with dishes from the restaurant menu or specialties prepared to order paired with appropriate wines.

Depending on type and size of group (minimum of 10) can design menus for $5, $10, $15 or $20 per person. Hors d'oeuvre menus range from $3 and $5 to $10 per person.

★ Can prepare dishes to special diet requests such as broth cooking instead of stir-frying.

EMPRESS OF CHINA

Empress of China
5419A FM 1960 West
Champions Village III
Houston, Texas 77069
583-8021

Four Seasons
Hotel-Houston Center

The Four Seasons Hotel is known for standard-setting food and impeccable service — from 24-hour room service for guests to conferences and catered events for thousands.

After it opened in 1982, the hotel quickly established itself as a center for fine dining, cultural organization events, charity benefits, weddings and holiday parties.

The hotel has earned Mobil's Four-Star designation, and the American Automobile Association gave both the hotel and its DeVille restaurant the AAA Four-Diamond rating.

Cultural centers, such as The Wortham Theater Center, Alley Theatre and Jones Hall, are only a few blocks away, and the Four Seasons is just across the street from Houston's major meeting facility, the George R. Brown Convention Center.

The Four Seasons has been host to many exceptional catered events from the opening of The Challenger Center to a private dinner for two in the Presidential Suite. The hotel has catered such diverse parties as a St. Patrick's Day reception for 600 and the Mayor's Ball in 1988 honoring Australia at the Houston International Festival.

The hotel also is known for hosting fine food and wine events. They include an annual tasting of Bordeaux wines, Evening of the Masters Cystic Fibrosis benefit and the Share Our Strength tasting that benefits various end-hunger organizations.

Catering managers are trained to plan parties from A to Z and can even serve as complete wedding consultants.

Hotel restaurant and catering menus reflect the creativity of talented young executive chef, Robert McGrath. He was on the American Culinary Federation's U.S. Culinary team in 1986 and was named one of America's Ten Best New Chefs in 1988. He was one of three chefs for two official dinners hosted by President George Bush during the 1990 Economic Summit.

DeVille, the hotel's luxury restaurant, is a showcase for McGrath's cuisine, which blends the best, freshest regional ingredients with innovative cooking techniques and concern for health and nutrition. Health-promoting alternative menus offer calorie- and fat-controlled dishes with gourmet flair.

Star Attractions

★ Full service facility from a coffee for 20 people to a benefit gala for 1,000.

★ Various dining and meeting facilities including the Terrace Cafe and lobby lounge featuring live entertainment.

★ Poolside dining through room service or pool cafe. Year-round swim club memberships available through the hotel sales department.

★ Complimentary courtesy car service in the downtown area.

★ Philosophy of supporting Houston civic and cultural groups and contributing food for the hungry through the Food Loop program of the End Hunger Network.

★ Almost all specialties, including smoked meats and fish, are prepared on the premises—a wide variety of excellent breads, sausages, pates, smoked bacon, salamis, ham, smoked salmon, custom desserts, pastries and ice creams.

★ Delivery to nearby offices (service fee is 16 percent).

★ Sunday brunch, which includes a large selection of a la carte entrees, appetizer bar, salad and seafood buffets and desserts.

★ In addition to Alternative Menus, the hotel offers special dietary requests, kosher service and vegetarian plates.

Catering Star Attractions

★ Full service catering in-house or off-site, from dinner for two to wedding packages and events for thousands.

★ Individualized service and high-quality food.

★ "White glove service," including all waiters; distinctive china and glassware for groups up to 100, special staffing considerations, bottled water, tablecloths and choice of 16 or 17 special napkin folds, and napkin change during the meal.

White glove service is automatic on any menu over $50 per person, but can be requested for an additional service charge.

★ Menus planned by catering manager and nationally recognized executive chef.

★ Theme parties and receptions. Variety of food stations throughout the room. Wait staff can dress in costume, and props are used throughout at no additional cost if hotel stocks necessary items.

For a Mexican party, the wait staff wears sombreros, ponchos and authentic Mexican attire; food stations include cabrito, fajitas and made-to-order tacos.

Props for an Oriental buffet include lanterns, umbrellas and Chinese war dog figures; food stations include stir-fry and tempura.

For an Italian theme party, the wait staff dresses in black and white; food stations include antipasto (all sausages and pates made in-house), pasta and carved meats.

★ Only hotel system that will substitute, at no cost, a particular entree if a guest at a function is not pleased with the dish. (For example, if a guest had salmon for lunch and salmon is the entree when he attends an event at the Four Seasons that evening, the wait captain will bring him a different entree of his choice.)

★ Simultaneous service for round tables of eight at no additional cost.

★ An event host is charged only one fee; it includes food, beverage, tax and gratuity. Only additional cost would be for audio visual equipment.

★ No-charge features if requested: house flowers for all bud vases; 18-inch mirrors for round tables; choice of votive or tapered candles; floor-length satin underliners (peach and pearl colors).

★ Office catering off-site for groups of 50 or more. A 48-hour lead time is preferred. Additional charges are made if a truck, tent or other rented items are used by the hotel.

Char Su Beef Tenderloin with Jack Daniels Barbecue Sauce and Smoked Corn Salad

Created by Four Seasons executive chef Robert McGrath for a benefit for the late cooking great, James Beard. The marinade can be used with other meats, poultry and fish such as fresh tuna.

- 4 (6½-ounce) beef tenderloin filets
- ½ cup Char Su Marinade (recipe follows)
- 1 to 2 cups Smoked Corn Salad (recipe follows)
- 1 cup Jack Daniels Barbecue Sauce (recipe follows)
- 6 ounces sugar snap peas, snow peas or fresh green beans
- ¼ teaspoon crushed Chinese dried red chilies

Marinate filets 2½ to 3 hours in the Char Su mixture. Grill to desired temperature. While meat is cooking, quickly saute the peas and dried chilies. Pour sauce over the plate, arrange the filet over it and garnish plate with Smoked Corn Salad and peas.

Serves 4

Char-Su Marinade
- 3 garlic cloves, chopped
- 1 teaspoon each: salt and fresh lemon juice
- 1 tablespoon each: peanut oil and honey
- 2 tablespoons sherry
- 3 tablespoons each: hoisin sauce and soy sauce

Mix ingredients thoroughly.

Smoked Corn Salad
- 2 ears sweet corn, smoked if possible or grilled in the husks, then cut off the cob
- 1 tablespoon chopped garlic
- ½ medium red onion, chopped
- ¼ small or medium jalapeno, seeded and chopped
- ¼ red bell pepper, chopped
- 1 teaspoon butter
- 1 medium potato, baked, peeled and cut in ½-inch dice
- ½ cup cooked black beans
- 2 tablespoons rice wine vinegar

Saute garlic, onion and peppers in butter in skillet. Add corn; saute 1 minute. Add potato, black beans and vinegar; saute 30 to 45 seconds. Season to taste and keep in a warm (not hot) place.

🍎 Good healthy recipe—only 11 percent of calories from fat.

Jack Daniels Barbecue Sauce
- 1 tablespoon peanut oil
- 1 tablespoon chopped garlic
- 1 large white onion, chopped
- 4 ounces Jack Daniels whiskey
- 1 tablespoon brown sugar
- ½ cup (4 ounces) veal demi-glace (see Special Helps section) or concentrated beef broth or brown sauce (made from mix)
- 4 ounces bottled or prepared barbecue sauce

Heat oil in a skillet and saute garlic and onion until soft. Deglaze pan with Jack Daniels (see Deglazing in Special Helps section if necessary) and let simmer until reduced by half.

Add brown sugar and let simmer 2 to 2½ minutes over moderate heat. Add barbecue sauce and demi-glace. Simmer 5 to 7 minutes; strain. Store in refrigerator. Use with meats, poultry or full-flavored fish such as fresh tuna.

🍎 Cut portion size of beef to 4 ounces; use 1 tablespoon of oil, ½ tablespoon in marinade and ½ tablespoon in barbecue sauce; omit salt.

Lemon Meringue Tart with Raspberry Coulis

1⅓ cups lard (solid white animal fat) or vegetable shortening
2 cups all-purpose flour
1 tablespoon salt
1 tablespoon sugar
⅔ cup ice water

Lightly rub lard, flour, salt and sugar together with fingers until crumbled to the size of peas. Pour water in center of mixture and incorporate quickly with hands. Do not overmix. Flatten to a disc and refrigerate 1 hour. Roll out into 2 (9-inch) pie shells and bake "blind."

To bake blind: Fit pastry into pie shells. Line insides of shells with aluminum foil; fill with dried beans or rice. Bake at 375 or 400 degrees until golden brown, 10 to 12 minutes. Remove beans (they can be reused for same purpose), remove foil and bake a few minutes until pastry is evenly cooked.

Lemon Filling
½ cup heavy (whipping) cream (see Special Helps section)
Juice and grated rind of 2 lemons
5 eggs, lightly beaten
1 cup sugar

Whip cream in a stainless steel or glass bowl and refrigerate. Combine lemon juice and rind with eggs and sugar in the top of a double boiler over simmering water.

Whip to make a sabayon (creamy thickened sauce) that increases three times in volume. Let cool. Lightly fold in whipped cream. Fill pie or tart shells; chill.

1 cup egg whites (8 large eggs)
1 cup powdered sugar
Juice of 1 lemon
½ teaspoon vanilla

With clean beaters and bowl, whip egg whites until frothy. Gradually add sugar and beat to firm peaks. Stir in lemon and vanilla. Spread on top of chilled lemon tart. Place under broiler 30 seconds, to color meringue, but do not let filling heat. Chill immediately.

Raspberry Coulis
1 pint raspberries
1 tablespoon sugar
1 tablespoon corn syrup

Combine berries, sugar and corn syrup in blender and blend until smooth. Strain to remove raspberry seeds. Ladle 1½ ounces on each dessert plate. Add a slice of lemon tart. Serve immediately.

Serves 8 to 10.

Four Seasons Hotel
HOUSTON CENTER

Four Seasons Hotel-Houston Center
1300 Lamar
Houston, Texas 77010
650-1300

JAGS

J AGS is a chic contemporary lunch-only restaurant in the Decorative Center featuring provocative food for people of discriminating taste.

It was opened in 1989 as an extension of Jackson Hicks' catering operation, Jackson and Company.

By day, the neutral white, gray and black color scheme, skylights, sheer white Austrian drapes and swagging, thriving plants and a fountain pool give the space the ambiance of an oasis. For private catered events in the evening, the mood is easily transformed with lighting, colors, decorations, flowers, music and entertainment. The area accommodates from 120 for lunch to as many as 1,000 for a reception and 500 to 600 for a black-tie dinner.

Jackson's "Manifesto" characterizes the caterer's philosophy about food and entertaining:

*If it isn't fresh, it isn't at JAGS; food should mirror the season.

Only the best is good enough for Hicks, who sets the standards for many of his food purveyors.

The menus and cooking style say "today;" but even when the food is trend-setting it is never bizarre. Jackson may serve a straight-forward chocolate mousse, but will present it artfully in a small clear glass flower pot centered with a real tulip.

Instead of a heavy cream sauce, a pan-seared salmon fillet may be napped with a light dill sauce or sprightly salsa.

*You eat with your eyes first. Exacting attention is paid to color, tablesettings, presentation and garnishes. (An example, a popular menu item, Chicken Taj, comes with the usual condiments for curry but they are arranged like colorful ribbons on the plate.)

*Nutrition is not a four-letter word. The JAGS staff is happy to meet special diet requests.

*Good food and good conversation are a part of good living.

Star Attractions

★ Sophisticated but casual multilevel setting with interesting architecture, fountain pool and skylights. The setting reflects the good design, furniture and fabrics displayed throughout the Decorative Center building.

★ Presentation — Contemporary china, service ware and garnishes (such as crisscrossed slivers of lemon peel over fresh asparagus) bear the stamp of Hicks' impeccable taste.

★ Specialties such as Blini Santa Fe, Smoked Capon on Cayenne Pasta, low-fat entrees, Tudor Salad (spinach, apples, Stilton and pecans), Lemon Velvet JAGS and Miss Ida's famous pies and cakes. The pecan and peach pies and fruit cobblers are legendary, but so are Miss Ida's carrot cake and chocolate cake garnished with pecan halves dipped in chocolate.

Malachite Soup — cream of potato and leek soup swirled with basil to resemble malachite. Served at President Bush's official luncheon during the economic summit.

Gazpacho Rio Grande

5 large ripe tomatoes (about 2¼ pounds), peeled, seeded and chopped
1 large cucumber (about 1 pound), peeled, seeded and chopped
½ cup chopped green pepper
1 large ripe avocado, peeled and diced (reserve seed)
5 tablespoons sherry wine vinegar
2 tablespoons fresh lime juice
1½ cups good quality tomato juice
2 teaspoons grated onion
½ teaspoon dill weed
½ teaspoon bottled liquid hot red pepper sauce (or more to taste)
Freshly ground black pepper and salt to taste (add salt after gazpacho is chilled)
⅛ cup extra-virgin olive oil
Sour cream and fresh dill weed for garnish

Combine tomatoes, cucumber, green pepper, avocado, wine vinegar, lime juice, tomato juice, onion, dill weed, pepper sauce, black pepper and oil. Leave avocado seed in soup to keep avocado from turning brown. Chill at least 24 hours.

When ready to serve, discard avocado seed, place soup in bowls and garnish with a dollop of sour cream and sprig of dill.

Makes 6 to 8 large servings.

Omit olive oil and sour cream; use only ½ avocado.

East/West Salad

2 cups cooked wild rice
1 cup cooked brown rice
1 cup cooked barley
1 cup soaked bulgur (cracked wheat)
1 cup toasted pecan halves
1¼ cups fresh corn kernels, sauteed or steamed
1 large tomato, peeled, seeded and chopped
1 bunch green onions, chopped (including green tops)
½ bunch fresh parsley
Dressing (recipe follows)
Chilled mixed salad greens

Combine rices, barley, bulgur, pecans, corn, tomato, green onions and parsley. Mix with dressing. Serve on a bed of chilled crisp mixed salad greens.

Serves 8 to 10.

Dressing
1 cup rice vinegar
½ cup peanut oil
Salt to taste

Combine ingredients and whisk until mixed.

Reduce nuts to ½ cup, peanut oil to ¼ cup. This is a good complex-carbohydrate, low-fat salad.

Jackson and Company

Jackson Hicks is the master of the grand event — the catered extravaganza.

After a ten-year apprenticeship in the specialty wine and food business after he graduated from Baylor University, Jackson perceived a need for catered productions on a grand scale. To fill that need, he started Jackson and Company in 1981 and has built it into one of the most prestigious, innovative catering firms in the country.

He has organized hundreds of major social and corporate affairs and fine arts benefits, and his planning notebooks, which meticulously detail every facet of an event, are sometimes several inches thick.

Jackson and Company is known for anticipating clients' needs and pampering guests with the best—from eclectic food, beautiful settings and flowers to polished, attentive service.

Among his credits are the ball for the Centennial of the Texas Capitol in Austin in 1988, 45 separate events for a corporate client during the Winter Olympics in 1988 in Calgary, Ontario, Canada and official luncheons for international leaders at the 1990 Economic Summit of Industrialized Nations here.

He and his staff have performed near-miracles in producing parties in Texas' most elegant homes, at ranches all over the Southwest, in museums and in plantation-like tents set up in unlikely places.

Among the most significant:

*A cocktail reception for 3,500, seated dinner for 650 and a series of dinners and receptions for the opening of the Menil Museum in Houston in 1987.

*The 1990 Economic Summit of Industrialized Nations—Mediafest reception for 5,000, which took place simultaneously in four Houston museums; official luncheons hosted by President George Bush, treasury secretary Nicholas Brady and secretary of state James Baker, and catering for two pavilions at the President's thank-you party for 15,000 on the grounds of the University of Houston.

*Seated dinner for 550 for the inaugural gala for the Watergarden at the Art Museum of South Texas in Corpus Christi in 1988.

*Luncheon, reception and seated dinner for the Museum of Modern Art in New York;

*One of a series of regional dinners hosted by the Wall Street Journal honoring the publication's 100th anniversary.

*Seated luncheons and receptions for President George Bush, the president of Italy and the Duchess of York;

*Seated dinner for 800 for the Museum of Fine Arts ball;

*Brunch for 2,500 guests at the Astrohall hosted by Turner Broadcasting, and a post-game cocktail reception for 4,000 at the Astrohall for the National Basketball Association All-Star weekend.

*Corporate events for international CEOs, openings in Houston of the Boehm Collection, Gucci, Guerlain of Paris, Krizia Boutique, Ungaro Boutique, Saks Pavilion, David Webb, Cartier, Tiffany and Company, Macy's and Neiman Marcus.

One of Jackson and Company's most challenging events was the inaugural gala for the Wortham Theater Center in May, 1988. After a champagne and hors d'oeuvres reception for 2,500 guests, Hicks directed a staff of 450 who cleared and reset the scene for a seated dinner for 1,500 in less than two hours.

Catering Star Attractions

★ A reputation for efficiently organized and flawlessly executed events, especially parties with thousands of guests. Plans for seating arrangements and location of food stations are often as detailed as blueprints.

★ Imaginative themes. For the Texas Capitol Centennial, Jackson and Company researched the history and used architectural elements in designs for invitations, menus and decorations. The original chandelier from the Capitol rotunda was re-created in a 1½-ton flower arrangement that had to be hoisted in place.

★ Food with panache. For a New Year's party at home, Jackson gives simple holiday foods new presence — traditional good-luck black-eyed peas might be served in china demitasse cups from a pot on the kitchen range and accompanied by Tom Thumb-size jalapeno cornbread muffins and champagne.

Flower arrangements are color-coordinated with the food and mood — desserts might be arranged casually in one room where guests serve themselves, while in another room, smoked salmon omelets are prepared to order and served from silver trays.

★ Lagniappe or that little something extra. A typical Jackson touch is specially designed favors such as the kaleidoscopes he had Bausch & Lomb create for guest favors at the Wortham gala dinner (to represent the kaleidoscope of artistic events in the theater center) or the 150 custom shoulder bags with special logos given to the client's corporate guests at the Winter Olympics events Hicks catered.

Jackson Hicks' New Potato Salad

8 **pounds little red new potatoes, washed and boiled with skins on until tender but not falling apart**
2 **cups homemade mayonnaise (can use light mayonnaise)**
½ **cup German-style mustard**
¼ **cup chive or wine vinegar**
¼ **cup dried (or ½ cup fresh) dill**
½ **cup chopped pimiento**
¾ **cup diced white onion**
2 **bunches thinly sliced green onion (with tops)**
2 **cups diced green bell pepper**
¾ **cup sliced pitted black olives**
1 **cup finely chopped dill pickles**
Salt (optional) and cracked black pepper to taste
Chopped fresh parsley and julienned red bell peppers for garnish

For sauce, combine mayonnaise, mustard, vinegar, dill, pimiento, onion, green onion, green pepper, olives, pickles, salt and pepper while potatoes are cooking. Remove potatoes when done and slice in half if they are large.

While potatoes are still as warm as possible, pour the sauce ingredients over them and toss until potatoes are coated. May be served warm after 30 minutes or refrigerated for as long as two days. Before serving, sprinkle with chopped parsley and garnish with julienned red peppers.

Note: The secret to success with this recipe is to add the marinade while potatoes are still warm.

Use light mayonnaise; omit salt.

Texas Gulf Shrimp Remoulade

Boil a large pot of water containing shrimp boil seasoning (or salt, black pepper, cayenne, bay leaf, mustard seed, onion, garlic and seaweed). Drop in 24 giant shrimp (8 per pound) which have been cleaned and deveined (leave tails on). Cook only 1½ to 2 minutes, just until flesh is white. Overcooking makes shrimp stringy and tough. Drain immediately and cover with ice.

To serve: Place 4 shrimp on each plate and garnish with watercress and Remoulade Sauce.

Remoulade Sauce
- 1 **cup homemade mayonnaise**
- 1 **tablespoon Creole mustard**
- ¾ **teaspoon grated onion**
- 1 **tablespoon capers**
- 2 **teaspoons finely chopped fresh parsley**
- ½ **teaspoon each: chopped fresh tarragon and chervil**

Combine ingredients and refrigerate covered a few hours for flavors to blend. Makes a little more than 1 cup.

🍎 Substitute ½ cup light mayonnaise for 1 cup mayonnaise.

Grilled Baby Leg of Lamb

1   or more legs of lamb (each less than
    5 pounds if possible)
6   garlic cloves
    Juice of 12 lemons
¼   cup dried rosemary
½   cup olive oil
    Salt and pepper

Remove lamb from refrigerator 2 hours before grilling. Sliver 4 garlic cloves lengthwise and insert into lamb at random, but space evenly, piercing holes with thin, sharp knife.

Crush remaining garlic and rub lamb thoroughly. Rub with some of the lemon juice (reserve the rest) and pat rosemary all over the surface.

Combine reserved lemon juice with olive oil to baste lamb as it cooks. It may be roasted on a spit or grilled over coals to an internal temperature of 145 degrees; it should still be pink inside, not gray. Salt and pepper just before removing from grill. Let lamb cool about 10 or 15 minutes before carving.

Serves 8 to 10.

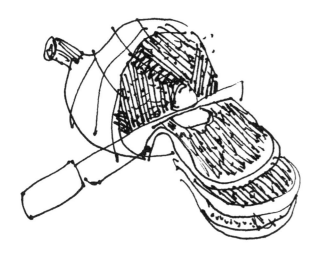

Texas Pecan Chocolate Mousse Cake

Created for a gala celebrating the centennial of the Texas Capitol building in 1988.

1   chocolate layer cake baked in a
    deep 8-inch pan, cooled and cut into
    3 layers

Praline Mousse
¼   pound semisweet chocolate
2   cups plus 3 tablespoons heavy
    (whipping) cream
2   egg whites
¼   cup sugar
5   tablespoons praline liqueur
½   cup finely chopped pecans

In double boiler, stir to melt chocolate in 3 tablespoons cream. Put aside to cool.

Beat egg whites to soft peaks, then add sugar, a little at a time, beating meringue into stiff peaks. Fold meringue into cooled chocolate mixture.

Whip remaining cream flavored with 2 tablespoons praline liqueur until stiff. Fold whipped cream gently into above mixture. When completely mixed, gently fold in chopped pecans.

Place bottom layer of cake on work surface; brush with 1 tablespoon praline liqueur. Top with half the mousse. Repeat with second layer of cake and remainder of mousse. Top with third layer of cake and brush top with final tablespoon of liqueur.

Refrigerate at least 1 hour to set. Ice with your favorite chocolate frosting and top with fresh roses.

JAGS
5120 Woodway at Sage (Decorative Center)
Houston, Texas 77056
621-4765

Jackson and Company
5120 Woodway at Sage
Houston, Texas 77056
523-5780

Melange Catering

& Gourmet To Go

Melange Catering & Gourmet To Go has set the table and the tone for hundreds of the city's most prestigious charity galas, balls and corporate events.

The company enjoys a four-star reputation for catering events of distinction, from a romantic dinner for two aboard a yacht to participating in a reception for about 15,000 for the 1990 Economic Summit of the World's Industrialized Nations.

Linda West, who opened Melange Catering in 1985, has more than 15 years experience in the catering business and has studied with some of the nation's finest chefs. In 1988, Sharon Graham and the staff of Graham Catering, a leading caterer in Houston since 1960, affiliated with Melange, expanding the company's capacity for full-service event planning.

Melange takes pride in offering a turn-key catering service that allows hosts to be guests at their own parties, whether they are entertaining with a small afternoon tea, a formal seated dinner or a large wedding reception.

Melange's attention to detail in service, menus and food preparation is as exacting for a Sunday breakfast in bed for one as for a major black-tie social event.

The growing list of Melange clients includes the Alley Theatre, Houston Ballet, Houston Grand Opera, Museum of Fine Arts, March of Dimes, Stehlin Foundation, Cystic Fibrosis Foundation, First City Bank, Dow Chemical and law firms Vinson & Elkins and Andrews & Kurth.

Over the years, the two caterers have been called upon to satisfy the tastes, personalities and special diet needs of some of the world's most discriminating celebrities — Mrs. Anwar El-Sadat, Ladybird Johnson, Shirley MacLaine, Robert Goulet, Sammy Davis Jr., Anthony Quinn, Ann Margret and Bob Hope.

One of the more challenging requests came from actor Richard Harris who asked for a fish and vegetable menu, but stipulated that only lunar and solar vegetables be served — lunar vegetables that have their growing period at night served for the evening meal, and solar vegetables that grow during the day served for the noon meal.

The Gourmet To Go department of Melange offers a variety of gourmet foods to pick up for busy days when you don't have time to cook — and for impromptu as well as planned entertaining from picnics at the beach to light, **heart-healthy dinners.**

Enjoy preparing some of Melange's most-requested recipes from recent events and menus.

Catering Star Attractions

★ Turn-key catering service — Melange can handle everything from invitations and place cards to rentals, valet parking and entertainment.

★ Finest food and service for a reasonable price (deposit required to book events). Free first consultation; one invoice for all services. Corporate billing available.

★ Custom menus for cocktail receptions, corporate meetings, board luncheons, box lunches, dinner parties, picnics, tailgate and boat parties.

★ Signature dishes including:
Cocktail Buffet specialties:
Caviar Roulade — egg souffle roll filled with caviar and frosted with sour cream (must be ordered at least two days in advance). Also smoked salmon and shrimp roulades;

Raspberry Cheese Torte (Cheddar cheese, ground pecans and onion molded and topped with raspberry preserves);

Turkey Melange (breast meat sliced and arranged on tray; breast reformed with turkey salad);

Pork Tenderloin with raspberry-flavored barbecue sauce.

Fine dining entrees such as:
Veal Riviera
Chicken Simon with Wine Sauce (boneless chicken breast stuffed with spinach, red bell peppers and pine nuts bound with cream);

★ **Luncheon entrees** including;
Chicken Enchiladas Verdes;
Chicken Salad Melange made with white breast meat only and sour cream mayonnaise dressing.
Caesar Salad (made with special Caesar dressing, homemade herb bread croutons and shredded fresh Parmesan; tossed just before serving);

Delectable desserts including:
Lemon Roulade with Raspberry Sauce
Chocolate Decadence and Kahlua Brownies made with special confectioners' chocolate ordered from Pennsylvania;
Bread Pudding with Whiskey Sauce

★ Box lunches that include choice of sandwich, salad and dessert.

★ Shop that features an array of sandwiches, salads, fresh soups and sweets as well as Gourmet To Go specialties. Open Tuesday through Friday from 9 a.m. to 7 p.m.; Saturday from 9 a.m. to 3 p.m. Closed Sunday and Monday.

★ Make specific soups to order with 24-hour notice.

★ Delivery available for nominal charge within a limited area.

Mélange
catering & gourmet to go

Gazpacho Blanca

☆
Cool, refreshing "starter" for a business luncheon.

3   medium cucumbers, peeled and seeded
3   cups chicken broth
3   cups sour cream (or 2 cups sour cream and 1 cup plain yogurt)
3   tablespoons white vinegar
2   teaspoons salt
2   garlic cloves, crushed

Condiments
4   medium tomatoes, peeled, seeded and chopped
¾   cup toasted sliced or chopped almonds
½   cup sliced scallions
¼   cup chopped fresh parsley
    Fresh cilantro sprigs (optional)

Coarsely cut cucumbers. Process in food processor with a pulsing motion until chunky. Mix with broth, sour cream, vinegar, salt and garlic in glass or non-metallic bowl. Chill thoroughly — best if done the day before.

When ready to serve, place soup in chilled bowls. Serve condiments in small bowls so guests can take their choice. Garnish with fresh cilantro if desired.

Serves 6 to 8.

🍎 Substitute 3 cups non-fat yogurt for sour cream.

Torte Melange

Featured entree from a Museum of Fine Arts Docents' luncheon.

This is an excellent party dish because it can be made ahead several days and frozen, or made one day ahead and refrigerated. Amounts for filling are not crucial — you can use less cheese and ham or substitute another favorite cheese such as Jarlsberg for swiss or substitute smoked turkey for ham.

1	**(17 ½-ounce) package frozen puff pastry sheets**
¾	**cup dry bread crumbs**
1	**pound sliced ham (honey-glazed, boiled or baked)**
2	**(10-ounce) packages frozen chopped spinach, thawed and thoroughly drained on paper towels**
1	**pound swiss, Jarlsberg or other favorite cheese, sliced**
4	**leeks, washed well, trimmed and sliced in ½-inch pieces (green and white parts)**
2	**red bell peppers, cut into 1x½-inch pieces and steamed briefly in a little water until soft**
1	**egg mixed with 1 teaspoon water (egg wash)**

Spray a 10-inch springform pan with non-stick coating spray. Roll out 1 thawed puff pastry sheet on a floured surface to measure about 16 inches square. Press into pan so sides and bottom are covered and there is about ¼-inch overhang. Sprinkle bottom with 2 tablespoons dry bread crumbs (they keep crust from getting soggy as torte bakes).

Over crumbs, layer: one-fourth of the ham, one-fourth of the spinach, 2 tablespoons bread crumbs, one-fourth of the cheese, one-fourth of the leeks, 2 tablespoons bread crumbs.

Then layer one-fourth of the ham, half the red pepper, one-fourth of the cheese slices, one-fourth the spinach and remaining red pepper.

Finally, layer remaining ham, leeks, bread crumbs, spinach, cheese and leeks. Sprinkle with bread crumbs.

Roll second sheet of puff pastry to a 20x16-inch rectangle. Place springform pan on top of pastry and with point of a knife, trace around shape. Remove pan. Cut circle about ¼-inch larger than tracing.

Brush rim of pastry with egg wash. Arrange pastry over top of torte, folding top crust over bottom at edges and pinching together to seal. Crimp or scallop edge to make a decorative rim. Brush egg wash around edge of top crust with pastry brush.

With a sharp knife, lightly score top for 8 wedges (can score for 10 pieces if you cut the baked torte carefully with a very sharp knife, but more than 8 pieces are harder to cut neatly).

With a sharp knife, cut stems, flat flowers and leaves from remaining pastry. Or cut 1-inch strips of dough and roll from end into rose shapes, stretching the edges gently as you roll to form petals.

Cut thin strips for stems; cut leaf shapes and score with knife tip to look like leaves. Brush top of pastry with remaining egg wash.

Place decoration pieces on top and brush with egg. Cut several slits in center of pastry (along lines already scored) to allow steam to escape.

Bake at 400 degrees 30 minutes. Cover loosely with a piece of foil and continue baking until brown, about 45 minutes. Let stand at least 30 minutes before serving. Serve warm or at room temperature.

Serves 8 to 10.

Refrigerate leftovers and warm to room temperature before serving.

Note: If desired, tint part of the dough with cake decorating food coloring or icing colors. Mix each color with egg white and beat with a fork. May be refrigerated overnight; let sit about 1 hour to warm before baking.

🍎 Use ½ pound part-skim milk cheese and 96 or 98 percent fat-free ham.

Sharon Graham's Gourmet Lite Dining Chicken Tetrazzini

One of six choices for the diet conscious.

2¾ pounds cooked chicken tenders or boneless chicken breast chunks
8 ounces dried fettuccine pasta about 8 inches long
½ cup finely chopped white onion
½ cup finely chopped green bell pepper
1 cup sliced medium mushrooms
1 cup chicken broth
½ cup all-purpose flour
½ cup cold water
3½ cups skim or low-fat milk
½ tablespoon (1½ teaspoons) chicken flavor base (recipe developed with Knorr)
1 teaspoon Worcestershire sauce
6 ounces pasteurized processed cheese spread loaf

Cook fettuccine in a large pot of boiling salted water following package directions. Saute onion, bell pepper and mushrooms in a little chicken broth. Mix flour and water and whisk until smooth. Mix milk, remaining broth, chicken flavor base, Worcestershire and flour-water mixture in a 4-quart saucepan. Add sauteed vegetables. Cook over low to medium heat until thick.

Cut cheese in chunks and add to sauce; let simmer, whisking occasionally, until cheese melts and sauce is thick enough to coat a spoon. Mix sauce, cooked chicken and fettuccine and turn into 3-quart casserole. Bake at 350 degrees about 20 minutes or until bubbly and heated through. Each 8-ounce serving provides 300 calories, 6 grams fat, 365 mg sodium and 78 mg cholesterol.

Can be frozen. If so, to reheat, thaw first in the refrigerator overnight. Remove cover, wrap in foil and place on baking sheet. Reheat at 350 degrees until bubbly and heated through.
Serves 12.

🍎 This is a low-fat, low-sodium recipe.

Gloria's Chicken

Named for a long-time friend of Linda West, this casserole is a classic at Melange Catering.

4 boned, skinned chicken breasts
Salt, white pepper and lemon juice
1 (10¾-ounce) can condensed cream of mushroom soup (preferably low-sodium type)
1½ cups real mayonnaise (Hellman's recommended)
1½ cups diagonally sliced celery
1 (5-ounce) can sliced water chestnuts
1½ cups dry cornbread stuffing mix (Pepperidge Farm recommended)
¼ cup melted butter
Salt, white pepper and bottled liquid hot red pepper sauce to taste
Chopped fresh parsley

Sprinkle chicken breasts with salt, white pepper and lemon juice and bake, covered, in 325-degree oven until done. Or cook in microwave. Cut or pull into small chunks.

Add condensed soup, mayonnaise, celery and water chestnuts. Spread evenly in 11x8½-inch dish, sprinkle with chopped parsley and bake at 350 degrees until heated through, about 30 minutes.

Makes 6 to 8 servings.

🍎 To reduce fat, substitute 1 cup light mayonnaise for regular and ¼ cup soft tub margarine for butter.

Ribs With Ginger Marinade

 Served at an outdoor engagement party for 150 guests.

- 2 racks (14 ribs each) baby back ribs
- ½ cup dark brown sugar
- 1 cup rum
- 1 cup lime juice
- 4 teaspoons chopped garlic
- 2 teaspoons ground ginger
- 1 cup soy sauce
  Pinch of salt and pepper

For marinade: In small bowl, combine sugar, rum, lime juice, garlic, ginger, soy sauce and salt and pepper; mix well. Brush generously on ribs, loin or other meats, wrap tightly in plastic wrap or bag and marinate in the refrigerator at least 4 hours or as long as 24.

Bake, covered with marinade, about 1 hour at 350 degrees. Remove meat from marinade and place ribs on a rack for 10 minutes at 400 degrees or over a hot grill 10 to 15 minutes to brown.

Serves 6 to 8.

Low-fat marinade, but high in sodium. To reduce sodium, omit salt and use low-sodium soy sauce.

Praline Spice Cake

☆ **Especially created by Linda West for the River Oaks Garden Club**

Deliciously simple; few will guess it starts with a mix.

- 1 (2-layer-size) spice cake mix
  Caramel Frosting (recipe follows)
  Praline Topping (recipe follows)

Bake cake according to package directions for a single layer, rectangular cake. If you don't have a 17x12 ½-inch pan, use a jellyroll pan or shallow 3-quart oven-proof glass pan (cake will be thicker so adjust baking time).

Caramel Frosting
- ½ cup butter
- 1 cup firmly packed dark brown sugar
- ¼ teaspoon salt
- ¼ cup milk
- 2 cups powdered sugar

Melt butter in 2-quart saucepan over low heat. Stir in sugar and salt. Bring to a boil over medium heat; boil hard 2 minutes, stirring constantly with a wooden spoon. Remove from heat. Stir in milk. Return pan to heat and bring to a full boil. Remove from heat and cool to lukewarm. Stir in powdered sugar gradually and beat until smooth. If too thick, beat in a little milk.

Praline Topping
- ¾ cup evaporated milk
- 1 pound brown sugar
- 2 tablespoons butter
- ¼ teaspoon salt
- 2 cups pecan pieces
- 1 tablespoon vanilla

In heavy 3-quart saucepan, combine evaporated milk, sugar, butter, salt and pecans. Bring to a soft ball stage (238 on a candy thermometer) over medium heat, stirring. Remove from heat. Add vanilla; let sit 5 minutes. Beat with a spoon by hand until mixture loses its gloss. Work quickly.

Cover a shallow jellyroll pan with parchment paper or wax paper. Pour praline mixture onto pan and let cool. When completely cool and hard, crumble by hand and sprinkle over top of frosting. Cut in squares to serve.

Menus from Melange

Luncheon for River Oaks Garden Club for 150 Guests

Chicken Barcelona

Mexican Melon Salad

Baby Lettuce, Radicchio and
Endive with Basil Vinaigrette

Dill Biscuits with Butter Rosettes

☆ Praline Spice Cake with Caramel Frosting ☆

Engagement Party for 150 Guests

Fresh Vegetable and Cheese Fondue

Avocado Halves with Black Bean Salad

Mesquite Rib Eye Medallions on Biscuits with
Horseradish Cream and Texas Salsa

Shrimp and Scallop Tempura with
Ginger Dipping Sauce

Grilled Chicken Kabobs

☆ Baby Back Ribs with Ginger Marinade ☆

Strawberry Baskets Romanoff

Apricot Almond Brie with Ginger Snaps

Business Luncheon

☆ Gazpacho Blanca ☆

Grilled Chicken Southwest with Texas Salsa

Avocado Halves with Black Bean Salad

Miniature Corn Muffins

Flan with Strawberry Garnish

☆ These recipes are included in Melange Section

Harris County Heritage Society Gala for 650 Guests
in Sam Houston Park

COCKTAIL RECEPTION MENU

Peppered Beef Tenderloin Cubes with
Horseradish Sauce

Shrimp and Potato Fritters with
Pickapeppa Sauce

Fresh Vegetables with Green Remoulade
and Dill Dips

Caviar New Potatoes with Garnish

DINNER MENU

Miniature Jalapeno Muffins and
Sour Cream Crescents

Chicken Duxelles with Madeira Sauce
Dirty Rice

Green Bean and Red Pepper Bundles

Biscuits and Cream Gravy

Bread Pudding with Whiskey Sauce

Dinner for Ten

Shrimp and Angel Hair Pasta

Chicken Simon with Wine Sauce

Vegetables Melange

Grilled Rosemary Potatoes

Sour Cream Crescent Rolls

Mocha Roulade with Chocolate Sauce

Melange Catering & Gourmet To Go
1000 Campbell Rd., Suite 400
Houston, Texas 77055
465-0077

Ninfa's

Since Ninfa's humble beginning as a 10-table taqueria near the Ship Channel in 1973, it has grown into a chain of 12 restaurants, 14 Bambolino's Italian Restaurants and four Atchafalaya River Restaurants with annual sales of more than $20 million.

The inspiration behind this business success story is Ninfa Laurenzo, who had been recently widowed in 1973 and had as assets five children, a capacity for organization and hard work, inexhaustible energy and $16 cash.

Ninfa's is famous for home-style regional Mexican food, which is different from Tex-Mex. Among Ninfa's signature dishes are avocado green sauce, Tacos al Carbon (now trademarked Tacos a la Ninfa) and Ninfaritas, a potent version of the Margarita cocktail.

Star Attractions

★ Eleven convenient locations in Houston including the original Ninfa's, 2704 Navigation. One restaurant in Dallas.

★ Festive atmosphere for birthdays, other special occasions or impromptu parties — bright colors, small fountain patios in some restaurants, rustic tables and chairs, colorful banners and parrot logo, which symbolizes love.

★ Authentic regional home-style Mexican cooking. Specialties include Ninfa's Green Sauce, a smooth dipping sauce of avocados, sour cream and tomatillos; fajita nachos; Queso a la Parrilla, a melted white cheese, mushroom, onion and pepper dish prepared as it is in Parilla, Mexico; carnitas, bits of boneless roast pork served with green and red sauces, and fajitas with marinated onions, pico de gallo and handmade tortillas.

★ Women making flour tortillas by hand on comals (griddles) in the dining rooms.

★ Some light dishes are available and small or half portions of selected dishes may be ordered.

★ Happy hour with free buffet at three locations — Gulf Freeway, Kirby at Richmond and Westheimer.

Chili con Queso

Ingredients as listed are for a medium amount that serves 6 to 8; ingredients in parentheses are for a large amount that will serve 12 to 15; the method is the same.

2	cups milk (4 cups)
1	cup half-and-half (2 cups)
3	pounds pasteurized processed cheese spread loaf (6 pounds), cut in chunks
¾	pound grated Cheddar cheese (1½ pounds)
1½	ounces each: finely chopped celery and bell pepper (3 ounces each)
1	teaspoon finely diced jalapenos, or to taste (2 ounces)
2	cups pico de gallo (4 cups)

Set up a double boiler with a pot inside a larger pot of simmering water. Combine the milk, half-and-half and cheeses in the top pan, set over simmering water and cook, stirring occasionally, until cheese is melted, about 10 to 30 minutes depending on amount.

Add celery and bell pepper. Heat to simmering or about 150 degrees. Add jalapenos and pico de gallo and bring to a simmer again. Cook until smooth and thickened to dip consistency. Serves 6 to 8 or 12 to 15 depending on proportions used. Serve with tortilla chips.

Bistec a la Mexicana

6   ounces beef tenderloin medallions
1   teaspoon chopped fresh jalapenos
1   tablespoon melted butter
¼   cup diced onion
½   cup diced, seeded, ripe tomatoes
¼   teaspoon black pepper
¼   teaspoon chopped garlic
¼   teaspoon cominos (cumin seed)
1   teaspoon salt
1   lime wedge
½   cup cooked pinto beans
⅓   to ½ cup hot cooked rice

Fry the jalapenos in the butter in a skillet. Add the beef medallions, onion, tomatoes, pepper, garlic, cominos and salt and saute until meat is done as desired. Serve on a large plate with beans and rice. Garnish with lime wedge.

Serves 1.

🍎 Limit portion of beef to 3 ounces; saute peppers in a non-stick coating spray; omit salt. With beans and rice, this is a nutritious entree.

Chorizo

2¼ pounds boneless pork butt, cut in
    ⅜-inch dice
¼   cup white vinegar
1   teaspoon salt
1½ teaspoons garlic powder or to taste
1   teaspoon each: ground oregano,
    pepper and cominos or to taste
4   ancho chilies (dried poblano peppers)
½   cup water

Place diced pork in a pan. Add vinegar, salt, garlic powder, oregano, pepper and cominos. Mix spices thoroughly with pork. Add the ancho chile paste (see Note); mix thoroughly until chorizo is a uniform color. Stuff in natural casings if available, or form into patties. Saute in skillet.

Makes about 2½ pounds.

Note: To make ancho chile paste, simmer the chilies in boiling water to cover in covered pan. Drain and discard water. Pull stem out of chile; peel and seed; discard peel. Blend chile with enough water to make a paste in an electric blender.

🍎 Use lean pork; divide into 8 servings to reduce portion to four ounces.

Flan

This is so incredibly rich, a little goes a long way.

- **3 cups sugar**
- **12 eggs plus 10 egg yolks**
- **4 (14-ounce) cans sweetened condensed milk**
- **5 cups milk**
- **1 (8-ounce) package cream cheese, softened**
- **4 tablespoons pure vanilla extract**

Place a large baking pan on bottom rack of oven and add ¼ inch hot water. Preheat oven to 350 degrees 15 minutes.

Place sugar in a large saucepan. Let sugar cook over low heat until it browns and liquifies, stirring constantly.

Pour equal parts of sugar into 2 (2-inch deep) flan pans or 2 shallow 2-quart pans making sure sugar covers entire surface. Let sugar harden in pans, then refrigerate until needed.

In an electric blender or food processor combine eggs, egg yolks, sweetened condensed milk, milk, cream cheese and vanilla. Process at medium speed until smooth, about 8 to 10 minutes.

Pour an equal amount of flan into prepared pans. Set flan pans in larger pan of hot water in oven and cook 2 hours 15 minutes or until a knife inserted in center comes out clean. After 20 or 25 minutes cover pans with aluminum foil. Top of flan should be lightly browned. Remove from oven and from pan of water and refrigerate flan until cold. Slice each pan into 12 pieces.

Garnish as desired. In the restaurant, the flan is served with honey to pour over the top.

Serves 24.

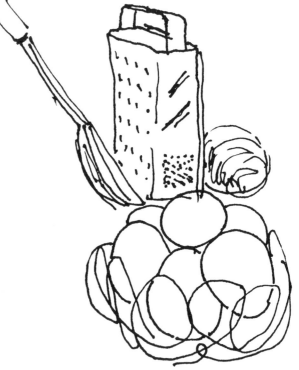

Atchafalaya River

Atchafalaya River Cafe helped put Cajun and Creole food on the culinary map in Houston.

Founded by restaurateur Richard Tanenbaum and his wife, Glenna, in 1985, Atchafalaya River is the namesake of a river in Louisiana Cajun country. The Tanenbaums' original recipes capitalized on the burgeoning trend for Cajun food nationwide.

Houstonians avidly took to the exciting dishes introduced by the Tanenbaums, and many local food critics and writers quickly recognized Atchafalaya River Cafe as a premier Cajun/Creole restaurant.

The two Atchafalaya River Cafes in Houston and two in Dallas have carried Cajun cooking far beyond its status as a fad.

Ninfa's organization purchased the Atchafalaya restaurants in November, 1989, and continues to develop new Cajun/Creole delights with the help of executive chef Jerry McClellan, a native Louisianian.

Ratatouille

1½	cups olive oil
2	pounds red onions, chopped
2	pounds each: green bell peppers, red bell peppers and eggplant
3	pounds zucchini
2	tablespoons chopped garlic
8	cups canned, drained tomatoes (reserve 4 cups juice)
2	tablespoons chopped basil
¼	cup Lawry's seasoned salt
2	tablespoons all-purpose Cajun seasoning (mixture of garlic, onion powder, basil, oregano, thyme, cayenne pepper, paprika, salt, cumin and black pepper)
2	tablespoons crushed black pepper
1	tablespoon cayenne pepper
2	pounds (26 to 30 count) boiled shrimp
2	gallons hot cooked yellow rice or Cajun dirty rice
	Freshly grated Parmesan cheese and chopped parsley for garnish

Heat oil in large pan such as a 2½-gallon braising pan. Add onion, bell peppers, eggplant, zucchini and garlic; saute 5 minutes. Add tomatoes, basil, salt, seasoning, pepper, reserved tomato liquid and cayenne. Bring to a boil and simmer 10 minutes. Remove from heat.

Do not overcook. Vegetables should still be bright, colorful and crisp-tender. Serve over rice; place boiled shrimp on top of vegetables.

Makes 2 gallons ratatouille; serves about 32.

Reduce oil to ½ cup; serve with ½ cup rice and 3 ounces boiled shrimp.

Sweet Potato Pecan Pie

Unbaked pastry for 2 (9- or 10-inch) pie shells
2 **pounds sweet potatoes, peeled, cut up and cooked**
1 **cup brown sugar**
½ **cup sugar**
4 **eggs**
½ **cup heavy (whipping) cream**
½ **cup butter, softened**
2 **tablespoons vanilla extract**
1 **teaspoon each: salt and ground cinnamon**
½ **teaspoon each: allspice and nutmeg**
Topping (recipe follows)

Remove bottom of springform pan and cut a round of dough to fit it. Place dough on bottom. Put pan side on and clamp spring. Cut 2 (10x½-inch) strips of dough and place around insides of pan pressing bottom edges together carefully to seal to dough on bottom. Repeat with second springform pan.

Beat potatoes in electric mixer until very smooth. Add brown sugar, sugar, lightly beaten eggs, cream, butter, vanilla, salt, cinnamon, allspice and nutmeg and beat on high speed of large mixer 5 minutes. Divide filling between prepared pans. Pour equal amounts of pecan topping over each pie.

Bake on middle rack of 325-degree oven until knife inserted in center comes out clean, about 1½ to 1¾ hours. In a convection oven, bake at 275 degrees about 1 hour 25 minutes. Cool at room temperature 30 minutes. Refrigerate until needed.

Topping
1 **cup sugar**
1 **cup dark corn syrup**
3 **eggs, lightly beaten**
2 **tablespoons melted butter**
1 **tablespoon vanilla**
⅛ **teaspoon each: salt and cinnamon**
2 **cups coarsely chopped pecans**

Combine sugar, corn syrup, eggs, butter, vanilla, salt and cinnamon in electric mixer bowl and beat on high speed until syrup is opaque, about 3 minutes. Stir in pecans. Set aside. Pour topping over each pie and bake as directed.

Each pie makes 10 servings.

Catering Star Attractions

★ Full service catering for corporate luncheons, company or family picnics, holidays, social events, graduations, weddings, birthdays and other special occasions. Can arrange for rentals, tents, decorations and entertainment such as mariachi musicians.

　　Have catered parties for Continental Airlines for 12,000 employees and guests at H & H Guest Ranch.

★ Special party menus for hors d'oeuvres, party and deli trays, barbecue, Mexican cocktails, beverage service and appetizers, Mexican dinner specialties and desserts.

★ Uses only USDA Choice meats, trimmed lean, specially seasoned and charbroiled.

★ Ninfa's Famous Fajita Fiesta — choice of beef, chicken or pork fajitas or a combination served with fresh, hot flour tortillas, marinated onions, rice, refried beans, red and green salsas, chile con queso, guacamole, pico de gallo and crispy tortilla chips. Free delivery in areas served by four Ninfa's restaurants — 3601 Kirby Drive at Richmond, 6154 Westheimer, 8507 Gulf Freeway and 9333-B Katy Freeway (Echo Lane).

★ Cater in or outside Houston; have catered parties as far away as North Carolina.

★ Frijoles a la charra or black bean soup substituted for refried beans at no additional cost.

Catering Star Attractions

★ Full-service catering with exciting New Orleans flair — can take care of part or all the arrangements for food, beverage service, special drinks, decorations, a Dixieland jazz band, jugglers and mimes.

★ Theme parties such as Crawfish Boil and "N'Awlins" Mardi Gras party.

★ Variety of hot or cold appetizers, grilled dinner entrees and desserts. Specialties include Shrimp Creole, Crawfish Etouffee, Crawfish Bisque, Jambalaya, Redfish Pontchartrain, two kinds of Creole Gumbo — seafood (oysters, shrimp and crab) and chicken-andouille sausage — Trout Tout Tout, Eggplant Chu Chu (stuffed with seafood), Red Beans and Rice. Desserts such as Bread Pudding (French bread, pears, peaches, apples, raisins and pecans) with a Peach Schnapps sauce and Peach Schnapps Chantilly cream.

★ Can do off-site catering in offices, businesses and in private homes.

Ninfa's - Atchafalaya River
6154B Westheimer
Houston, Texas 77057
977-4000

Post Oak Grill

Post Oak Grill is the latest venture of successful restaurateur-consultant Manfred Jachmich and partner, Ethel Hankamer, who also has years of experience in the restaurant business.

Jachmich, who comes from a restaurant family in Koblenz, Germany, apprenticed in Germany and Switzerland. He worked for several hotels and restaurants after he came to the United States in 1963.

In addition to managing the former Bismarck and owning restaurants — Ruggles, Ruggles II and Cafe Moustache — he has been in charge of food development for Continental and Eastern airlines.

His style of cooking is founded on solid European tradition, but he constantly changes his menus to keep Post Oak Grill in the culinary mainstream.

Because he has observed that today's customers are more sophisticated, more knowledgeable about food and more health conscious today, current emphasis is on a "cleaner cuisine," he said.

"We are using basic honest ingredients to produce basic, honest food," said Jachmich. "Everything is fresh and goes directly from the refrigerator to the skillet or grill to plate."

He also has lightened many traditional dishes and gladly accommodates guests' wishes and special dietary needs.

The restaurant has been extensively redesigned and redecorated; it seats 135 including the long front patio, but can accommodate 220 for private parties.

Although the setting is relatively casual, mahogany paneling, carpeting, multi-paned arched glass windows and comfortable raised banquettes defined by stylized flower arrangements in tall urns give it an air of understated elegance.

From the vantage point of the highest banquettes, the main dining area almost resembles a stage. Metal drop lights cast a flattering coppery glow over the setting at night.

The wall above the banquettes continues the theatrical motif. It is covered with murals of turn-of-the-century theater loges painted by Phyllis Bowman and Elva Stewart. The loges are peopled with characters who could have stepped right out of Toulouse Lautrec paintings.

Star Attractions

★ Contemporary menu emphasizes fresh ingredients and lighter cooking style.

★ Specialties including French Onion soup, Tuscan Chicken Soup, Goat Cheese Ravioli with 2 Sauces, Fried Calamari, Caesar Salad (try it topped with fried shrimp), Tomatoes Manfred (named for co-owner Manfred Jachmich), Ethel's Grilled Salmon Salad (named for co-owner Ethel Hankamer), Amy's Grilled Chicken with feta cheese (named for hostess Amy Way), triangle-shape potato pancakes with cheese and tomato relish;

Pastas such as angelhair with Roma tomatoes, garlic and basil;

Grilled entrees — fresh salmon, halibut, chicken breast, veal chops (range from about $11 to $16);

★ Appealing plate presentations;

★ Happy to accommodate special dietary requests;

★ Sunday brunch — 11 a.m. to 4 p.m. with special salads, egg dishes (Eggs Benedict, Eggs Your Way, omelets, Huevos Rancheros), Texas Pecan Waffle, Nova Scotia salmon and bagel, sandwiches and pasta dishes;

★ Well balanced wine list featuring champagnes, California, Italian and French wines. Wines by the glass.

Most of Post Oak Grill's menu items are available for catering. Jachmich has done benefits and arts parties, but he particularly enjoys catering to customers who live in the area and want to do a home-style meal with a minimum of fuss.

Food is arranged on large, distinctive platters that can go right to the table or buffet. Post Oak Grill also will take advance orders and prepare catered food for pick-up.

Tomatoes Manfred

12   Roma tomatoes, sliced ¼-inch thick
2   (14-ounce) cans hearts of palm, drained and cut into ½-inch pieces
½   cup Basil Vinaigrette (recipe follows)
½   medium red onion, minced
3   tablespoons chopped fresh basil
6   lemon wedges
6   sprigs parsley
2   pounds lump crabmeat (optional)

Form ring of tomatoes on large plate. Cut hearts of palm into pieces and place in middle of ring. Pour dressing over tomatoes and hearts of palm.

Sprinkle red onion and basil over tomatoes. Garnish with lemon wedge and parsley sprig.

Place crab on one side of plate or in a ring around tomatoes.

Serves 6.

Note: Store remaining Basil Vinaigrette in refrigerator.

Basil Vinaigrette
2   teaspoons Dijon mustard
2   tablespoons red wine vinegar
    Juice of 1 lemon
1   tablespoon minced fresh parsley
1   tablespoon chopped fresh basil
¼   teaspoon salt
    Pinch of white pepper
2   cups salad oil

Combine mustard, vinegar, lemon juice, parsley, basil, salt and pepper. Whisk oil slowly into dressing with a wire whip. Keep refrigerated. Do not make in food processor.

Use 1 cup oil and replace 2 tablespoons vinegar with 1 cup vinegar.

Shrimp Tampico

36   large raw shrimp (10 to 15 count per pound), cleaned and peeled; leave tails intact
2   tablespoons each: ground white, black and red pepper, dried oregano and garlic powder
¼   cup olive oil
10   tomatillos, husk and boil in water to cover until tender enough to pierce with a fork easily
3   jalapenos, cut in half lengthwise and seeded
1   bunch cilantro, chopped
1   pound regular rice
2   tablespoons butter

For seasoning: mix white, black and red peppers, oregano, garlic powder and ½ teaspoon salt. Dip shrimp into seasoning mixture.

Heat a large saute pan or skillet until very hot. Add olive oil and saute shrimp quickly over high heat, 2 minutes per side. Do not overcook. Remove shrimp from pan and keep warm.

For sauce: Mash tomatillos and mix with jalapenos, cilantro, salt and white pepper to taste. Cook rice. Add butter and salt to taste.

Place ¾ cup rice on each plate, arrange shrimp on rice and pour sauce over shrimp. Serve with fresh cooked vegetables.

Serves 6 to 8.

Reduce shrimp portion to 3 ounces; use only 4 tablespoons oil; omit butter from rice.

Trout Meuniere

6 (7- to 8-ounce) fresh skinless Gulf
    Trout fillets
2 eggs
1 teaspoon water
1 cup all-purpose flour
    Salt and white pepper
2 ounces (4 tablespoons) margarine
2 ounces vegetable oil
    Lemon Butter (recipe follows)

Beat eggs and water; set aside. Mix flour with 1 teaspoon salt and 1 teaspoon white pepper. Heat margarine and oil in a skillet. Dry trout fillets with paper towels. Dip each in seasoned flour and shake lightly to remove excess, then dip in egg mixture. Saute in hot skillet over high heat until the first side is brown. Turn fillet, reduce heat and cook until trout is done, about 3 to 5 minutes.

Serve with rice and fresh vegetables.

Serves 6.

Use egg substitute instead of eggs; spray pan with non-stick coating spray; omit butter sauce.

Lemon Butter
1 stick (8 tablespoons) butter, cut
    in chunks
    Juice of 2 lemons (about ¼ cup)
⅛ teaspoon Worcestershire sauce
    Salt and white pepper
    Chopped fresh parsley for garnish

Combine butter, lemon juice, Worcestershire, ½ teaspoon salt and a pinch of white pepper in saucepan and melt over low heat to a creamy consistency. Spoon butter over each trout fillet. Garnish with chopped parsley.

Tenderloin Emerson

1 (3- to 4-pound) beef tenderloin,
    trimmed
½ medium size yellow onion, chopped
1 tablespoon butter
2 pounds fresh spinach, well washed
    and cleaned
½ pound pinenuts (pignolia), roasted
    golden brown
½ teaspoon nutmeg
4 ounces heavy (whipping) cream
½ cup dry bread crumbs
    Salt, pepper and olive oil as needed

Saute onion in skillet in heated butter. Drop spinach into a pot of boiling water to blanch; drain. Add spinach to onion and cook quickly until tender (just takes a few minutes). Combine onion-spinach mixture, pine nuts, nutmeg, cream and bread crumbs.

Cut tenderloin lengthwise 2 inches deep. Fill with stuffing and tie with thin kitchen twine. Season tenderloin generously with salt and pepper; baste with olive oil.

Sear tenderloin in skillet over high heat to seal in juices. Transfer to 325- to 350-degree oven and roast 20 to 25 minutes for medium rare or 30 to 35 minutes for medium well.

Serve with roasted new potatoes and fresh vegetables.

Serves 6.

Note: To roast pine nuts—spread in one layer in a dry skillet and roast to light brown shaking skillet constantly.

Use ¼ pound pinenuts; substitute half-and-half for cream; do not baste meat with oil; limit portion of meat to 4 ounces.

English Trifle

- 6 **egg yolks, beaten**
- ½ **teaspoon vanilla extract**
- 1 **cup sugar plus 2 teaspoons**
- ¼ **cup all-purpose flour**
- 2 **cups milk, heated to a boil**
- 2 **(1-pound) Sara Lee frozen pound cakes, partially thawed**
- ½ **cup light Bacardi rum**
- ½ **cup brandy**
- 1 **quart whipping cream (chill cream, bowl and beaters well before beating)**
- 1 **(12-ounce) jar raspberry preserves (preferably seedless)**
- 1 **(8-ounce) pouch frozen blueberries**
- 1 **cup sliced almonds, toasted**

Make pastry cream: Thoroughly mix egg yolks, vanilla, ½ cup sugar and flour. Off heat, slowly pour hot milk, a little at a time, into egg mixture in a saucepan, whisking constantly.

Return to heat and bring to a boil for 2 to 3 minutes, whisking constantly until thickened to a custard consistency. Transfer to a bowl and sprinkle top with 2 teaspoons sugar to prevent a film forming on top. Refrigerate until thoroughly chilled.

Trim cakes to remove brown crusts. Slice each lengthwise into 4 layers. Sprinkle layers of one cake with rum; sprinkle other cake layers with brandy. Whip cream with remaining ½ cup sugar.

Assemble trifle in a glass bowl in the following manner:

Bottom layer—2 slices cake spread with one-fourth of preserves. Top with half of pastry cream.

Second layer—2 slices cake; one-fourth of preserves; half of whipped cream; half of frozen berries topped with half of toasted almonds.

Third layer—repeat bottom layer.

Fourth layer—repeat second layer, except use almonds and berries in a decorative fashion.

Serves 16.

Catering Star Attractions

★ Most any menu item available for catered events

★ Fill orders for take-out foods or can deliver catered food.

★ Specialties including pasta dishes, Lemon Pepper Chicken with spinach and pasta, and escargot with garlic-herb butter.

Post Oak Grill

Post Oak Grill
1415 S. Post Oak Lane
Houston, Texas 77056
993-9966

Rao's
Ristorante Italiano & Bar

Rao's blends the Italian appreciation of good food with the tradition of gracious hospitality.

Owner/chef Tony Rao (RAY-o), a native Houstonian, believes in lighter foods and sauces although his cooking is rooted in tradition. He updates his style and menu constantly with dishes and techniques he finds on trips to Italy.

Rao's travels have produced such signature dishes as his stellar version of Risotto alla Milanese served with Osso Buco, Chicken Involtini (chicken breast stuffed with Italian sausage and spinach), fresh pasta dishes and the latest "designer" vegetables from arugula and Tuscan beans to broccoli rabe and fennel.

The restaurant, which seats 225, opened in May, 1987, just north of the Southwest Freeway. Located between the Cashco Tower and Summit Plaza, Rao's is convenient to Greenway Plaza, the Summit, Galleria, Bellaire, the Texas Medical Center, River Oaks and West University Place.

A building within a building, it boasts unique architectural features — a skylight roof, glass windows framed by a contemporary version of Roman columns and, between the open, airy restaurant and the roof, the metal fretwork of a geodesic dome. A painted sea green archway defines dining areas and continues the cool color scheme of peach and sea green.

Dining areas on different levels are almost like stage sets lit by hanging fabric-covered parasol lamps. The main dining area offers a pleasant view of the fountain plaza between the Coastal and Summit towers across the street.

A new patio offers full food service. It faces Richmond Avenue and seats 50 at umbrella tables. Shrubs, colorful flowers and lighting make it a pleasant setting for dining.

Star Attractions

★ Conveniently located near the Summit in Greenway Plaza for before-event or before-game dining.

★ Great people-watching place. Rao's is frequented by the professional sports figures, power lunchers and celebrity performers.

Among them; Billy Gibbons of ZZ Top, Dan Fogelberg, Frankie Avalon; rock stars including the Rolling Stones, Rod Stewart, Fleetwood Mac and Pink Floyd; Joan Rivers; Dodgers' manager Tommy Lasorda; Oilers' general manager Mike Holovak and running backs Mike Rozier and Allen Pinkett; Rockets star center Akeem Olajuwon.

★ David Goldman, an experienced chef and graduate of the Culinary Institute of America, is second in command in Rao's kitchen. He makes the pastries and desserts.

★ Caesar salads made tableside — grilled chicken, boiled shrimp or lump crab added on request.

★ Specialties such as Snapper Toto with lump crab; Involtini di Pollo (stuffed chicken breasts), homemade pastas and risotto.

★ Dishes are cooked to order and the chef is happy to honor special diet or preparation requests.

★ Full service bar. Complimentary hors d'oeuvre at happy hour from 4 to 7 p.m. Monday through Friday.

★ Complimentary valet parking (there's a new circular driveway entrance on Richmond).

Rao's
Ristorante Italiano & Bar

Pureed Bean Soup with Pasta (Pasta di Fagioli alla Fiorentina)

Beans (recipe follows)
Sauce (recipe follows)
½   pound dried short tubular pasta such as ditalini
Coarse salt
Freshly ground black pepper
6   to 8 teaspoons olive oil (optional)

Beans

1   pound dried cannellini (white kidney beans)
Cold Water
5   large sage leaves (fresh or dried)
1   heaping teaspoon rosemary leaves (fresh or dried)
2   large garlic cloves, peeled
3   tablespoons olive oil

Soak beans in cold water to cover overnight. The next morning, preheat oven to 375 degrees. Drain beans and place in a medium casserole (preferably terra cotta or enamel) with the sage and rosemary leaves, garlic, oil and 6 cups cold water. Cover the casserole and bake until beans are very soft, about 2 hours.

When beans are done, prepare the sauce.

Sauce

2   medium garlic cloves, peeled
3   tablespoons olive oil
2   tablespoons tomato paste
½   teaspoon crushed red pepper flakes
1   teaspoon rosemary leaves (fresh or dried)
Salt and freshly ground pepper

Coarsely chop garlic. Heat oil in small saucepan over medium heat, add garlic and saute 2 minutes. Add tomato paste, red pepper flakes, rosemary and salt and pepper to taste.

Meanwhile, transfer casserole of beans from oven to top of range and place over medium heat. Remove cover, taste beans for salt and pepper and mix well. Add the sauce and simmer 10 minutes.

Remove as many rosemary leaves as possible then put bean mixture through food mill (using disc with smallest holes) or food processor. Place in a second 2-quart casserole and simmer over low heat 15 minutes. Taste and correct seasoning.

Bring a large pot of cold water to a boil. Add a little coarse salt, then drop in pasta and cook until al dente, 9 to 12 minutes depending on the brand of pasta. Drain pasta, then add to casserole and cook 1 minute more before serving.

Serves 4 to 6.

Notes: The bean puree can be prepared in advance and the pasta added at the last moment. If so, add broth to thin the puree because it will thicken as it stands. Serve with a twist of black pepper, and if you wish, a teaspoon of olive oil over each portion.

*Cannellini beans are available at food specialty shops, gourmet shops and some better supermarkets.

*Tony Rao preserves fresh sage and rosemary leaves in salt, a trick he learned from Italian cookbook author-teacher Guiliano Bugialli.

Layer the herb leaves with coarse salt and store in a sterilized, tightly closed jar at room temperature. Use within six months; wash before using.

Omit olive oil in beans and do not add oil to each portion before serving.

Pasta alla Vodka

6   quarts boiling water
    Coarse salt
1   pound penne pasta
6   or 7 tablespoons unsalted butter
½   teaspoon (or to taste) crushed
    red pepper flakes
1   cup less 2 tablespoons vodka
    (preferably Polish or Russian)
1   scant cup canned Italian plum
    tomatoes, drained and crushed
    with hands
1   scant cup heavy (whipping) cream
1   cup freshly grated Parmesan cheese

Bring water to a boil in a large pot; add 2 tablespoons coarse salt. Drop in pasta and cook until al dente (firm to the tooth). Meanwhile, warm bowl in which the pasta will be served.

For sauce, melt butter in a skillet large enough to hold the cooked pasta. Add pepper flakes and vodka; simmer 2 minutes. Add tomatoes and cream; simmer 5 minutes. Add 1 teaspoon coarse salt.

When pasta is done, drain well and pour into the skillet with the sauce; while it is simmering, add Parmesan and mix thoroughly. Pour into heated serving bowl and serve immediately.

Serves 4.

🍎 Substitute evaporated skim milk for cream and 3 tablespoons soft margarine for butter. Omit added salt for low-sodium.

Baked Snapper Genovese Style (Pesce Pagello al Forno con le Patate)

2 **(1-pound) snapper fillets or other firm white fleshed fish fillets with skins on**
1½ **pounds boiling potatoes**
⅔ **cup olive oil**
1 **tablespoon chopped garlic**
¼ **cup chopped fresh parsley**
Salt and freshly ground black pepper

Preheat oven to 450 degrees.

Peel potatoes and cut into very thin slices, only slightly thicker than potato chips. If they are too thick, they will not be done when they should. Wash in cold water, then pat dry thoroughly with cloth kitchen towels.

In a bowl, combine potato slices, half the olive oil, half the garlic, half the parsley and a liberal amount of salt and pepper. Mix thoroughly, then spread the potato slices evenly over bottom of a shallow 2-quart baking dish.

Place dish in the upper third of preheated 450-degree oven and bake until the potatoes are about half cooked, about 12 to 15 minutes.

Remove dish from oven and arrange fish fillets, skin side down, over potatoes.

Mix remaining oil, garlic and parsley in a small bowl and pour over fish, basting well. Sprinkle generously with salt and pepper. Return dish to oven.

After 10 minutes, remove from oven and baste fish and potatoes with some of the oil from the dish. Loosen potatoes that have become browned and stuck to the sides of the dish with a spatula, moving them away. Push into their places slices that are not so brown. Return dish to the oven and bake 5 more minutes.

Serve piping hot with all the pan juices, scraping loose any potatoes stuck to the dish. These are the most delectable bits so save them for yourself or someone you like nearly as well, said Rao.

Serves 4.

 Reduce oil to ¼ cup.

Veal Shanks Osso Buco with Risotto Milanese

> 4   **veal shanks, about 2 to 3 pounds with bone, cut into 1½-inch thick pieces**
>   **Flour**
> 3   **tablespoons olive oil**
> 1   **tablespoon safflower oil**
> 1   **medium onion, finely chopped**
> 1   **medium carrot, finely chopped**
> 1   **bay leaf**
> 1   **cup dry white wine**
> 1   **cup chopped fresh tomatoes**
>   **Salt and freshly ground pepper to taste**
>   **Beef or chicken stock (optional)**
>   **Gremolada (recipe follows)**

Dredge veal shanks with flour. Heat oils in a medium skillet or saucepan. Brown veal shanks over medium heat, turning until evenly browned. Remove from pan. Drain on paper towels. Heat oils in same pan and add onion; saute until translucent. Add carrot, bay leaf and wine. Cover and simmer over low heat until wine evaporates.

Return veal to pan and add tomatoes, salt and pepper; cover and cook over low to moderate heat, turning veal shanks occasionally. Add stock if more moisture is needed. Cook about 30 minutes.

Meanwhile, prepare the Gremolada.

Gremolada
> 2   **tablespoons minced Italian parsley**
> 1   **teaspoon minced garlic**
> 1   **tablespoon grated lemon rind**

Combine parsley, garlic and lemon rind.

When veal is done, uncover pan and sprinkle gremolada over veal shanks. Remove veal from pan, arrange on plates with Risotto Milanese around it.

Serves 4.

🍎 Because veal shanks are a higher fat meat, eliminate oils and saute vegetables in non-stick cooking spray.

Risotto Milanese

> 1   **tablespoon each: butter and safflower oil**
> 1   **medium onion, finely chopped**
> 1   **cup arborio rice**
> ½   **cup dry white wine**
> 2   **cups chicken broth or more as needed**
>   **Freshly ground black pepper to taste**
> ½   **teaspoon saffron**
> 1   **tablespoon butter**
> 2   **tablespoons freshly grated Parmesan**

Heat butter and oil in a heavy, medium saucepan; add onion. When it wilts, add rice. Cook several minutes, add wine and cook, stirring, until wine evaporates. Add broth, pepper and saffron, and cook until rice is tender, about 15 minutes, stirring almost constantly — don't leave the pot unattended for more than a minute, and add more broth as it is absorbed. Watch rice carefully so it doesn't burn. Taste for doneness, remove from heat and add 1 tablespoon butter and Parmesan.

Serves 4.

🍎 This recipe is only 25 percent fat calories even with the butter and oil.

Catering Star Attractions

★ Catering for groups of 50 to 500. Rao's has served and catered for celebrity performers including Michael Jackson (a vegetarian) and Frank Sinatra.

★ Private dining room upstairs for wedding rehearsals, receptions and other parties; seats 90.

★ Restaurant available for private parties on Sundays when it's closed.

★ Select menus for small to large groups (minimum order $35). Can provide service personnel, deliver orders ready to serve on trays or prepare orders for pickup at a designated time.

★ High quality, fresh ingredients from pastas to cheese and deli trays.

★ Will go to your home and cook for a group.

★ Extensive choice of pastas, meats, fish, salads, pizzas with assortment of fresh toppings, frittatas, side orders and dessert. Some samples:

Rao's Menu Selections for Catering

PASTA
Penne alla Vodka
Ravioli al Sugo
Tortellini Genovese
Lasagna
Cannelloni

Meats
Veal Marsala
Veal Parmigiana
Saltimbocca

Fish
Grilled salmon
Snapper Toto (a house specialty done with lightly sauteed salmon fillets topped with a sauce of crabmeat, pinenuts and wine)
Swordfish
Fresh tuna

Salads
Tomato/Avocado/Arugula
Radicchio
Spinach
Pasta

Cheese & Deli Tray
Wide variety of meats and cheeses
Fresh vegetable or fruit trays

Frittata/Quiche
Pasta Frittata
Carrot Frittata (made with egg whites)
Herb Frittata (fresh basil and mint)

SIDE ORDERS
Roasted potatoes
Fresh jumbo asparagus
Green beans with fresh tomato and basil
Fruit or vegetable salads

Sandwiches
Grilled chicken breast
Grilled fresh tuna
Meatball
Italian sausage and peppers
Baked eggplant

Desserts
Cannoli
Coconut pie
Raspberry tart
Chocolate mousse
Tiramisu (classic Italian dessert of ladyfingers, mascarpone double cream cheese, eggs, and chocolate)
Italian Cream Cake

Rao's Ristorante Italiano & Bar
#12 Greenway Plaza
Houston, Texas 77046
622-8245

Caterers

The Acute Catering Co.

Richard and Doreen Kaplan started Acute Catering in 1985, and the combination of their innovative food, unique themes, decorations, party sites and food presentation soon gained them the reputation of a catering company that exceeds expectations.

Helping establish and encourage Acute's reputation as one of Houston's premier catering firms were events as varied as a Galveston beach party, late night champagne birthday party, the grand opening of Hermes of Paris in Houston and the 1989 Houston Grand Opera Ball.

The Kaplans have a special sensitivity to client needs coupled with sophisticated ideas on cuisine and all the other elements necessary for memorable entertaining.

They believe that every party has its own personality, and they pride themselves on orchestrating the event to the client's wishes and mood whether it is a small intimate dinner or one of the grand galas of the social season.

The solid foundation for every Kaplan production is Richard Kaplan's classic training at the Restaurant School of Philadelphia, where he earned a culinary management degree, plus experience gained at some of the most exciting, trend-setting restaurants in the United States.

They include One Fifth in New York, where he was sous chef; Claire, a seafood restaurant on New York's trendy West Side, where as head chef Kaplan gained a reputation for excellence and originality, and La Terraza di Marti in Key West, where he was executive chef seven years.

He came to Houston in 1984 as head of the kitchen that earned the first critical acclaim for River Cafe on Montrose.

Among Richard Kaplan's signature dishes are "beggar's purses," small blini wrapped around fillings of caviar or fresh spinach and sundried tomatoes and tied with chives; Lacquered Duck, similar in presentation and taste to Peking Duck; "braided" salmon and sole, and the Tiffany Truffle, a rich white chocolate-raspberry truffle in a white chocolate Tiffany "bag" served with raspberry and Armagnac coulis and creme chantilly.

Quail in black pepper sauce and baby back ribs basted in tropical citrus juices were grilled over a mesquite fire for a party aboard the tall sailing ship Elissa in Galveston; the champagne birthday party guests enjoyed frozen orange souffle bon bons, bittersweet chocolate and mocha torte, mascarpone trifle and white chocolate and raspberry petits fours.

The 400 guests at the Hermes opening dined on braids of Norwegian salmon and lemon sole in a light ginger butter sauce. For the Opera Ball, Kaplan did lump crabmeat and caper petits fours, warm buckwheat pancakes topped with Ossetra caviar and "beggar's purses" of fresh spinach and sun dried tomatoes.

Doreen Kaplan brings a dynamic sense of presentation to menus chosen by clients. She often selects one-of-a-kind baskets or serving pieces designed by local artists and she concentrates on making each setting as pleasing to the eye as the food is to the palate.

The Kaplans insist on designing their own buffet tables with marble panels, glass bricks and even art works, and Doreen Kaplan pays as much attention to the arrangement of a simple fresh fruit compote as to a lavish display of fresh lobster.

For some parties, the Kaplans have designed special serving pieces and had them fabricated—such as the wrought iron-cast iron warming stands they use for parties with Southwestern, Tex-Mex or Mexican themes.

Having Acute cater your parties tells your guests you have arrived, and although Richard Kaplan handles gala benefit balls for 750 and luncheons for 1,000 in stride, he particularly enjoys serving dinner parties for 25 to 30. He loves the challenge of successfully pleasing distinguished clientele and celebrities with widely different personalities and entertaining needs.

Acute directed all catering activities for London-based British Petroleum during the 1989 Houston visit of Her Royal Highness The Duchess of York.

Acute has been the official caterer for the Houston Grand Opera since 1988, has catered a number of events for The House of Hermes and has catered a seated dinner for Unicef honoring actress Audrey Hepburn at the home of Baron and Baroness Enrico di Portanova.

During the 1990 Economic Summit of Industrialized Nations, Kaplan catered a seated dinner for 100 ambassadors and State Department guests at the Menil Museum for hosts, the Frederic Maleks. Mr. Malek was economic summit director.

Size does not indicate the importance of a party to the Kaplans.

"A small party is just as important to us as a large party; we give each our full attention," says Doreen Kaplan.

"We are blessed with a number of clients who entertain regularly and are very progressive in their menu planning," said Richard Kaplan. "It is a personal challenge to me to keep up with their culinary appetites, and it gives me a really good feeling to have clients trust me to carry out their innovative desires."

Seated Dinner for Unicef Honoring Audrey Hepburn
March 22, 1990

Braided Norwegian Salmon and Asparagus

Light Ginger Beurre Blanc

Pink Grapefruit-Peppercorn Sorbet on Japanese Greens Tossed with Virgin Olive Oil

1988 Joseph Phelps Chardonnay

Roasted Rack of Prime American Lamb on Potato Galette

Madeira Glace   Miniature Vegetables

1984 Edna Valley Pinot Noir

The Tiffany Truffle

1986 Piper Sonoma Brut

Opening Night Reception, Museum of Natural Science
January 8, 1990

Seafood Bar in "Kryptonite" Ice Carving

Ceviche in Scallop Shells
Oysters on the Half Shell
Fresh and Smoked Mussel Salad with Roasted Peppers

Smoked Beef Tenderloin Assortment of Breads

Shredded Quail and Wild Mushrooms in Puff Pastries with Roasted Garlic Glace

Saute of Snow Peas, Jicama, Red Peppers and Shiitake Mushrooms in Ginger and Soy

Veal and Smoked Vegetables Tortellini in a Black Pepper Pasta Sauteed Tableside in a Poblano Cream Sauce

Salmon and Scallop Gateaux in a Sour Cream and Dill Crust

Baby Carrots, Miniature Cauliflower and Yellow Squash

DESSERT TABLE

Chocolate Galaxy Centerpiece

Mocha Praline Asteroid Torte

Milky Way Torte

The Moon and the Stars — Hazelnut Meringue and Chocolate Tiles

Berries in the Clouds

Apple Streusel Space Bars

Moon Rocks – Chocolate Chip Cupcakes Filled with Cream Cheese and Chocolate Chips

Post-Opera Reception at
Wortham Theater Honoring
The Duchess of York
November 3, 1989

Boneless Duck Breast Stuffed
with Veal and Truffles

Tangerine Ginger Glace

1987 Alsace Willm Reisling

Baby White Asparagus on Fresh Spinach
Leaves with Stilton Cheese
and Walnut Vinaigrette

Grilled Cured Wild Salmon Scallops
on Wilted Watercress

Fresh Tomato Beurre Blanc

Garnish of Salmon Caviar

1985 Chateau de la Maltroye
Chassagne Montrachet

Miniature English Garden Cake

Veuve Clicquot Brut N.V.

Reception and Seated Dinner for 100,
Houston Economic Summit

RECEPTION

Squash Blossom and
Texas Goat Cheese Beignets

Wild Mushroom Feuillettes

Spicy Beef Tenderloin Tartare

DINNER

Grilled Lemon and Dill-Cured Wild Salmon
Served on a Bed of Wilted Watercress

Sauteed Scallops of Milk-Fed Veal
with Herbed Noodles

Concasse of Fresh Garden Vegetables
and Sauce Morilles

Salade of Oregon Field Lettuce –
Roasted Sweet Pepper Vinaigrette with
Baby Fennel and Chevre in a Hazelnut Crust

Pave of Bittersweet Chocolate – Toasted
Coconut Anglaise Sauce with
Raspberry Coulis and Creme Chantilly

Seated Dinner for 80 Honoring
Beverly Sills at the Home of
Mr. and Mrs. Jim Dawley
November 18, 1989

Smoked Vegetable Tortellini Wrapped
in Fresh Basil

Poached Shrimp with
Crawfish Mousse on Cucumber

Culbertson Brut N.V.

Saute of Plantains Topped
with Fresh American Caviar
and garnish of Creme Fraiche and Cilantro

1986 Drouhin Chablis

Salad of Field Greens and Edible Flowers
with Tarragon and Champagne Vinaigrette

Pink Grapefruit and Vodka Sorbet

Breast of Pheasant en Croute

Layered with Field Mushrooms and Foie Gras

Madeira Glace, Roasted Shallots,
Miniature Carrots and Asparagus

1979 Chateau Talbot St. Julien

1982 Silver Oak Cabernet Sauvignon

"La Cioccolata Sills" Pave
of Bittersweet Chocolate

Sauce Grand Marnier

Coffee

Dinner For 80 on The Tall Ship Elissa in Galveston

*Bacon Wrapped Boneless Chicken
Stuffed With Jalapeno*

*Black Bean, Cilantro and
Goat Cheese Chalupas*

Tiny Fajita "Purses"

DINNER

*Mesquite Grilled Smoked Quail Basted
in Barbecue Sauce*

Mesquite Grilled Marinated Baby Back Ribs

Poppyseed Yeast Rolls

*Blackened Rainbow Trout with
Lemon Caper Butter*

*Smoked Vegetable Tortellini Salad with
Fresh Peas and Tomatoes*

*Cold Grilled Green and Yellow Squash
in Garlic Mint Vinaigrette*

Roasted Corn and Pepper Chutney

Blackout Cake

Pecan Pie-Homemade Vanilla Ice Cream

Cinnamon Apple Cobbler

Private Cocktail Reception for 100

*Veal and Spinach Roulade
with Dijon Mayonnaise*

Wild Mushroom Feuillettes

Norwegian Salmon Tartare on Herb Croutons

Sevruga Caviar in Tiny Barquettes

*Smoked Breast of Quail with
Cumberland Glace and Brioche Toast*

Venison Pate   Duck and Goose Liver Pate

Miniature Stuffed Squash

Roasted Pepper Timbales

Grilled Sea Scallops with Cilantro Sauce

Dilled Shrimp Mousse and Cucumbers

Smoked Fish Terrine

*Veal Loin Stuffed with Sweetbreads
and Brandied Apricots*

Crawfish and Caper Saute

Miniature Tiramisu

White Chocolate and Raspberry Petits Fours

Assorted Fruit Tarts

THE ACUTE CATERING CO.

The Acute Catering Co.
2711 Kipling Street
Houston, Texas 77098
528-1133

A Fare Extraordinaire

A Fare Extraordinaire has an extensive repertoire of cooking styles and a flair for producing unforgettable parties.

Karen Lerner, who started the catering company in 1984, is known for attention to the details that make a party outstanding — from themes and decorations to valet service, flowers, beverage service, music and entertainment.

Lerner says that success depends on the ability to produce creative, memorable menus whether the occasion is an elegant after-the-opera dinner for eight or a festive Southwestern fete for 800. Consistency and high quality also are crucial, she says.

A Fare Extraordinaire caters events for groups of 20 to 3,000 for everything from dinner parties at home to corporate cocktail receptions, office parties, birthdays and anniversaries.

Lerner began doing catering on the side while working as a registered nurse, then joined former Houston caterer, Kay Kahle.

Lerner's services were soon in demand by such clients as Foley's, James Avery Craftsman, Texas Opera Theater, Houston Bar Association, Fulbright & Jaworski law firm, Museum of Fine Arts and Museum of Natural Science and Baylor College of Medicine.

She recently catered Rice University's thank-you lunch for 1,500 Rice faculty, staff members and volunteers involved in the 1990 economic summit.

Booking parties two to four weeks in advance is requested. Lerner can sometimes be more flexible except during busy seasons such as the summer and winter holidays.

Lerner charges no consultation fee; prices are based on per-person charges. Extras include flowers, entertainment (such as arranging for a harpist, pianist or tarot card reader), staffing, beverage service, rentals, invitations or accepting R.S.V.P.s for invitations.

Chef Jill Cucchiara attributes success to the young and energetic professionally trained kitchen and wait service staff. They take pride in what they are doing and try to be creative and health conscious, too, says Cucchiara.

"We not only have fun, we really love this profession," she said.

Star Attractions

★ Personal service

★ Exciting food such as oven-dried Roma tomatoes piped with Texas goat cheese and fresh herbs, scallion crepes rolled with smoked chicken and fresh kumquats and lace cookie tacos filled with chocolate mousse and fresh berries accompanied by three sauces.

★ Imaginative young chef from California, Jill Cucchiara, a graduate of the Culinary Institute of America.

★ Custom orders for pick-ups (Lerner prefers one week's notice).

★ Known for fresh-baked breads such as fennel beer bread, Italian flat bread and savory jalapeno scones.

★ Finishing touches such as hand-crafted pinatas filled with pralines for a Mexican fiesta party or making French Provincial chair covers and linens for a French country picnic. Exotic tropical drinks, a 25-foot poor boy sandwich or old bath tubs filled with glass bottle Cokes are other attention getters.

Sour Cherry Relish

1	medium white onion, minced
1	pound fresh cherries, pitted and quartered
	Olive oil to saute
½	cup sugar or more depending on tartness of cherries
¼	cup champagne vinegar
¼	cup white wine

Lightly saute onion and cherries in a little olive oil in skillet 5 minutes. Add sugar, vinegar and wine. Cook over medium heat 10 to 15 minutes. Cool and serve.

 Good, low-fat sauce.

Scallion Crepes

2½ cups milk
1   cup all-purpose flour
2   green onions, cut in 1-inch pieces
1   teaspoon salt
2   tablespoons melted butter
3   eggs

Combine milk, flour, onions, salt, butter and eggs in electric blender and blend until pureed. Batter should be light green in color. Heat crepe pan over medium heat. Lightly oil pan between making each crepe.

Using a 2-ounce ladle, pour batter in pan and swirl to cover bottom. Cook 3 to 4 minutes, or until crepe begins to loosen from sides. Turn out on parchment or foil and layer between each crepe. Cut each into eighths, fill with desired filling and roll up.

Makes 18 to 20 (5-inch) crepes.

Peppermint Cream

4   cups milk
1   bunch fresh peppermint, cleaned
6   tablespoons sugar
8   egg yolks, lightly beaten
1   vanilla bean

Scald milk with peppermint (heat until bubbles form at edges) in a 1½-quart saucepan. Mix sugar and egg yolks in a separate bowl. Pour scalded milk over sugar mixture and return to the pot. Add vanilla. Cook over low heat 10 to 15 minutes, stirring constantly until thickened to sauce consistency. Do not boil.

Strain and refrigerate at least 3 hours. Serve with cakes or fresh fruit.

Makes about 5 to 6 cups.

A Fare Extraordinaire
4509 Kelvin
Houston, Texas 77005
527-8288

Menus

APPETIZERS:

Crostini (fried appetizer sandwich) with Grilled Quail Salad and Cranberry Relish

Country Rabbit Terrine with Mango Chutney and Cornichons

Lemon Sorbet

DINNER:

Australian Lamb Chops with Crushed Peppercorns and Mint Roasted Creamer Potatoes with Venison Sausage and Fresh Thyme

ACCOMPANIMENT:

Herb-Roasted Eggplant, Squash and Multicolored Bell Peppers

DESSERTS:

Pecan Shortcakes with Poached Anjou Pears and Vanilla Bean Cream Sauce

Apple Bavarian Tartlets

White Chocolate Raviolis Filled with Chocolate Hazelnut Mousse and an Amaretto Cream

DINNER BUFFET

Hors d'oeuvres

English Cucumber and Scallion Crepes with Fresh Dill

Baked Polenta with Gorgonzola Cheese and Spicy Walnuts

Marinated, Grilled Loin of Veal with Sour Cherry Relish

Peppercorn Poached Salmon with Lemon Rind Relish

Celery Root and Bell Pepper Salad with Champagne Vinaigrette

Spinach and Goat Cheese Brioche Pies

Chocolate Hazelnut Terrine with Peppermint Cream

Byron Franklin

Byron Franklin started his catering company about 12 years ago after friends, including the late Wendy Haskell Meyer, editor of Houston Home & Garden at the time, encouraged him to share the kind of entertaining he did at home with others. Although many people think of him as a pastry chef, because of his training in Europe, he defines his services and staff as "the personal valets of the 90s."

He provides complete catering, specializing in fine food, flexible services and personal attention from an efficient staff. Franklin has catered everything from hors d'oeuvres for a small dinner party to a four-course buffet for 2,000. He and his staff can manage every detail from rental services, flowers, decorations, tenting, special lighting and valet parking to professional kitchen staff.

Franklin, who is from Baytown, had a Fulbright grant to the Academy of Music in Vienna, Austria, and returned there to live for six more years.

Vienna provided the perfect introduction to fine pastry-making. He apprenticed at the famous Marschfelderhof restaurant where he perfected regional Austrian pastries such as Johann Strauss Torte, Apple Strudel and Mohr im Hemd, individual chocolate pastries.

When he returned to Houston, he balanced his food preparation with vocal coaching positions at Rice University and Houston Baptist University. But catering clients soon demanded most of his time, and he started the business in 1978.

He also supplied pastries to Rainbow Lodge (the popular walnut pie, for example) and to Neiman Marcus-Town and Country, Marshall Fields, the Lancaster Grille, Cafe Alley at the Alley Theatre and the former SRO, where Ruggles owner/chef Bruce Molzan first made his imprint on the Houston culinary scene.

Memorable parties are the result of planning and practice, says Franklin, who takes pride in discovering the perfect culinary match for every occasion. He creates food that tastes as good as it looks, and he and his staff smooth the way for clients to enjoy their roles as hosts.

Franklin works on a contract basis, but does not charge an initial consultation fee. At his first meeting with the client, they set parameters for budget, determine the services needed, purpose of the event and the client's particular likes and dislikes.

Franklin submits a proposal, which is usually discussed and adjusted to satisfy both client and caterer.

Establishing a budget is very important. Once it is decided, a deposit serves as a reservation for the event date.

For large events, the deposit is usually broken down into three or four payments, which are due as the work progresses, Franklin says. He follows this routine, even for small parties, unless the client says, "Just take care of it."

Catering tends to be a very personal service, one that depends on rapport with the client; discerning clients do not simply shop the Yellow Pages, Franklin says. He believes that most successful caterers build their businesses on referrals from satisfied clients.

Star Attractions

★ Complete catering service from an experienced host and caterer who knows how to bring all the elements of an event together successfully.

★ Varied menus from international cuisines and skillfully recreated dishes from many cultures.

★ Outstanding assortment of desserts from classic Austrian pastries to downhome favorites.

BYRON
FRANKLIN
C A T E R I N G INC.

Apple Strudel

Dough

- ¾ cup lukewarm water
- 1 large egg, lightly beaten
- ¼ teaspoon white vinegar
- 2 tablespoons butter, melted
- 2½ cups bread flour
  Melted butter and dry cake crumbs (sponge cake) for assembly

Combine water, egg, vinegar and butter. Add flour all at once and mix by hand until dough forms a ball. Transfer to floured surface; knead 10 minutes. Again form dough into a ball and let rest on a floured surface under a heated metal or earthenware bowl 10 minutes (dough should remain warm so it is elastic).

Filling

- 3 pounds large tart green apples (such as Granny Smiths), peeled, cored and sliced
- ½ cup sugar
- 1 cup brown sugar
- 1 cup dry cake crumbs (from genoise or other plain cake)
- ½ cup dark rum
- 2 teaspoons cinnamon
- 1 cup seedless white (golden) raisins
- ¾ cup chopped walnuts

Combine apples, sugars, cake crumbs, rum, cinnamon, raisins and walnuts in large mixing bowl. Set aside for flavors to meld thoroughly.

Assembly

Cover a large (about 6x4-foot) table with a tablecloth and generously flour it. Place warm dough in the center of the table, dust lightly with flour and roll out gently to ⅛-inch thick. With the backs of your hands, working your way around the table, quickly stretch and pull the dough until it is paper-thin and covers the table. Pinch back together if dough should tear.

Brush the stretched dough (it will hang over table edges) with melted butter and sprinkle the surface with reserved cake crumbs. With a sharp knife trim the excess dough around the table edge. Place filling along one of the short edges within 2 inches of each end. Lift the table cloth and use it to roll the dough around the filling, jelly-roll fashion. Brush the top with melted butter and place, seam side down, on a baking sheet.

Bake at 450 degrees 10 minutes, reduce oven temperature to 400 degrees and butter the top of the dough. Continue baking 20 minutes or until strudel is golden brown, brushing the top again with butter after 10 minutes.

Remove from oven and let strudel rest 20 minutes before cutting. Serve with whipped cream (schlagobers).

 Good, low-fat dessert, but high in sugar.

Dinner for Australian Ambassador
Home of the Australian Consul
General Peter Urban, 1990

Bay Scallop Mousse with Red Pepper Sauce

Toast

*Grilled Tenderloin of Beef
with Horseradish Cream*

Roasted New Potatoes in Five-Pepper Butter

Artichoke Bottom Stuffed with Spinach Souffle

Braised Baby Carrots and Squash

Herbed Cheese Rolls

*Watercress, Arugula and
Romaine Lettuce Salad*

Honey Dijon Vinaigrette

Imperial Chocolate Bombe

Byron Franklin
1318 E. 29th
Houston, Texas 77009
864-4342

DELICATEXAS
Food Creations & Catering

In less than a year, DELICATEXAS has expanded the horizons of fine catering in the Houston area.

The catering company and shop in Kingwood is a forerunner of the 1990s concept of offering gourmet and healthful take-out foods.

DELICATEXAS is the fulfillment of a long-time dream of chef Peter Rosenberg and his wife Rosemary; it became a reality in January, 1990, after months of planning with business partner, Greg Nakanishi, formerly with Tenneco.

Rosenberg earned a reputation for creative cuisine as executive chef at several of the most prestigious luxury hotels in the country — the internationally recognized Hotel Bel Air in Los Angeles, the Mansion on Turtle Creek in Dallas and the Remington on Post Oak Park, now the Ritz-Carlton Houston.

Rosenberg began training at 14 in Rhodesia where he learned formal "silver service" while working in a hotel and restaurant. He graduated from the Culinary Institute of America in Hyde Park, New York, where he began to formulate his philosophy of combining the best seasonal products and a light regional style with classic techniques.

At the Remington, he cooked for royalty, celebrities and corporate tycoons, and often catered formal dinners in the homes of admiring customers, preparing the distinctive cuisine for which the hotel was known.

Rosenberg quickly realized that in-home catering met several needs, chiefly that hosts could relax and enjoy entertaining at home but still impress guests with a five-star meal.

He also saw a need for gourmet take-out food. DELICATEXAS meets those two challenges by providing expert personal service and a product of superb quality and freshness.

DELICATEXAS prides itself on flexibility in designing menus and services which meet the specific requirements of each customer, even for heart-healthy or other special diets.

At the take-out location, 15 minutes north of Houston Intercontinental Airport, DELICATEXAS offers customers a health-conscious alternative to cooking at home.

The menu of fresh entrees and soups changes weekly and take-out dishes are conveniently packaged to heat in the microwave or oven at home.

Add a fresh salad from an array available daily, and a dessert from the weekly selection, and you have a gourmet meal in minutes. Another asset is that each person can have his or her favorite dish without the cook having to prepare separate meals.

DELICATEXAS also offers cooking lessons, food styling, consulting, and due to the proximity to Intercontinental Airport, custom cuisine for corporate jet travel.

The interior of the shop was designed by Rosenberg to include a streamlined, efficient professional kitchen, which enables DELICATEXAS to handle catering assignments of most any size. The storefront presents a modern, sophisticated showcase for weekly take-out specials.

A "Wall of Fame" displays articles from various newspapers and magazines honoring Rosenberg's accomplishments in the culinary field. There you will read about the dinner he catered for the French delegation planning participation in the 1990 Economic Summit of Industrialized Nations and a food presentation and lunch he did for the Texas Beef Industry Council and American Cancer Society at a seminar in Austin.

For the seminar, "Strategic Decisions — The Great Texas Food Fight Against Cancer," he devised a safer technique for smoking and grilling meats that retains the flavor but avoids the possible carcinogens associated with smoking and grilling meats.

Rosenberg also completed the Pritikin Restaurant Certification Program, which highlights diet, fitness and health awareness, and he can provide heart-healthy gourmet dishes.

DELICATEXAS presented grilled specialties as one of the caterers for President George Bush's thank-you party for about 15,000 guests after the economic summit.

DELICATEXAS SAMPLE MENUS

APPETIZERS

Hot

Blackened Catfish Fingers with
Creole Mustard

Grilled Honey-Glazed Shrimp

Ginger Duck Skewers

Vegetable Tempura with
Horseradish-Mustard Glaze

Cold

Smoked Chicken Jicama Skewers

Vegetable Sushi with Mushroom Soy

Avocado and Crab Meat Tartlet

Cucumber with Sour Cream and Caviar

BREAKFAST

Seasonal Selection of Fresh Squeezed
Fruit Juices

Almond-Raisin Cheese Blintz with
Hazelnut Syrup and Maple Cream

Huevos Ranchero with Homemade Chorizo

BRUNCH

Sliced Seasonal Fruit and Berries

Norwegian Salmon Poached in Aromatics
with Asparagus and Caviar

Creme Brulee

Tortilla Soup

Grilled Chicken Caesar Salad with
Shredded Monterey Jack Cheese

Chocolate Pecan Tart

LUNCH

She Crab Soup

Roast Cajun Beef Tenderloin with
Three Salads

Lemon Tart with Fresh Berries

Garden Green with Chardonnay Fresh
Herb Vinaigrette

Hickory Smoked Chicken, Jalapeno Pasta
and Southwest Vegetables

White Chocolate Cheesecake

DINNER

Risotto Cakes with Porcini Mushroom Sauce
and Fresh Thyme

Passion Fruit Sorbet

Roast Pheasant with Spicy Golden Pear Sauce
and Corn Fritters

Chocolate Chocolate Mousse Cake with
Fresh Raspberries

Asparagus and Tomato Bisque with
Blue Cheese

Grilled Gulf Red Snapper
with Ginger Sherry Sauce

Grapefruit Sorbet

Veal Medallions with Stonecracked Mustard
and Lemon Thyme Sauce

Blueberry Buckle with Vanilla Ice Cream

DELICATEXAS

Food Creations / Catering

DELICATEXAS Food Creations & Catering
2624 Chestnut Ridge Drive
Kingwood, Texas 77339
358-1800

How Sweet It Is

How Sweet It Is catering began with a cheesecake recipe.

Jill Roman was the manager of the first wine bar in Houston, and when the owner wanted to serve cheesecake, Roman said she had a great recipe. She volunteered to bake the cheesecakes, and soon realized that she would rather be making cheesecakes than working in the restaurant. She left and started How Sweet It Is about 10 years ago.

At first Roman made cheesecakes for a few restaurants, but soon she was supplying more than 50 hotels and restaurants with cheesecakes in every imaginable flavor — more than 45.

As her reputation for custom cheesecakes grew, Roman expanded the business to other cakes and desserts, then to full-fledged catering.

Having lived in Indonesia, Jamaica, the United States, Canada, England and France while she was growing up, Roman takes a worldly, and sometimes cross-cultural, approach to food.

However, a party has to have more than just good food to be successful, she says. She believes a good party results from paying attention to details, and that creativity and sensitivity to hosts and guests combine to produce memorable entertaining.

Among her signature touches are the use of handmade copper trays, lavishly garnished trays and the imaginative use of fresh flower garnishes such as tiny sweetheart roses garnishing a white chocolate hazelnut praline cheesecake.

Her eye for detail sets Roman's work apart — the textures, colors and tastes combine to make each menu unique whether it is a brunch, cocktail reception or seated dinner.

Guests are more comfortable if the menu includes some items that people are familiar with, she says, but Roman also believes in introducing people to something new.

"We are the only baker in town that makes wedding cheesecakes — tiered, stacked, square or round — iced with a delicious white chocolate cream cheese icing," said Roman. How Sweet It Is also does groom's cheesecakes.

Heart-shaped cheesecakes with cherry or strawberry topping are the most popular cakes year 'round, especially for Valentine's Day and Mother's Day, she says.

Cheesecakes can be delivered almost anywhere, and, with one day's notice, Roman will ship them overnight anywhere in North America.

Star Attractions

★ Can provide staff and take care of rental and delivery, decorations, tableware, flowers and music for parties of different sizes.

★ Known for special touches, such as: Waiters costumed as railroad conductors for a party aboard a train; customized cookies — sugar cookies hand-painted with appropriate slogans, such as "Get them to the church on time" for a pre-wedding party.

As a memento for honorees at a 40th anniversary party held in the Gem and Mineral Exhibit area at the Museum of Natural Science Roman had custom-made oversized buttons designed saying "Forty's a Gem."

★ Custom cheesecakes. Suggest a favorite flavor and, if Roman doesn't have a recipe, she can usually create one.

★ Providing ample food. "I think I'm a Jewish mother at heart so I always prepare extra."

★ Seated luncheon for 230 hosted by KRIV-TV (Channel 26).

★ Seated dinner for 250 for Baylor College of Medicine, Texas Children's Hospital at the Museum of Fine Arts.

★ Assembled 180 food gift boxes of food gifts for a corporate client and had them delivered by tuxedoed waiters to people on the client's gift list recipients every six weeks for a four-night period.

Nanaimo Bars

This favorite Canadian cookie always makes a hit at parties.

Bottom Layer
- ½ cup butter
- ¼ cup sugar
- ⅓ cup unsweetened cocoa powder
- 1 teaspoon vanilla
- 1 egg, beaten
- 1 cup unsweetened coconut
- 2 cups graham cracker crumbs
- ½ cup chopped walnuts

Melt butter in saucepan over low heat. Add sugar, cocoa, vanilla and egg. Cook, stirring, over medium heat until the mixture thickens.

Remove from heat and stir in coconut, crumbs and walnuts. Pat firmly into a butterd 13x9x2-inch glass pan. Refrigerate at least 1 hour.

Filling
- ¼ cup butter
- 2 tablespoons milk
- 2 tablespoons egg custard mix powder (such as Jell-O Americana Golden Egg Custard)
- 2 cups sifted powdered sugar

Cream butter. Beat in the milk, custard powder and powdered sugar. If mixture is too thick to spread, add a few more drops of milk. Spread over bottom layer and refrigerate 30 minutes or until firm.

Topping
- 4 ounces unsweetened or semisweet chocolate
- 1 tablespoon butter

Melt chocolate and butter in a dish set over hot water (or in microwave — see Special Helps section). Spread over the filling. Before chocolate hardens completely, cut into squares. Refrigerate at least 1 hour.

Best Darn Margaritas

These margaritas live up to their name.

- 1 liter best quality tequila
- ⅓ liter Triple Sec
- 4 ounces creme de cacao
  Juice of 6 to 10 limes
- 4 to 6 ounces bottled lime juice (Preferably Rose's)
- 25 to 30 ounces sweet/sour mix

Mix tequila, Triple Sec, creme de cacao, lime juice and sweet/sour mix; serve over ice or blend to a slush in blender with crushed ice. Makes 20 to 25 (4-ounce) drinks.

For a salt rimmed glass: Rub the rim of each cocktail glass with a lime wedge to moisten and dip rim into plate of salt.

Best Darn Margarita for One

- 1½ ounces best quality tequila
- ¼ to ½ ounce Triple Sec
  Juice of 1 lime
  Splash of creme de cacao
- 2 ounces sweet/sour mix
- ½ ounce bottled lime juice

Mix ingredients and serve over ice or blend as described above.

How Sweet It Is
946 Heights Blvd. at 10th Street
Houston, Texas 77008
880-0038

Jalapeños
Seafood-Mexican Cocina & Cantina

Jalapeños has fiesta, will travel.

Owners Tomas and Sue Romero and their experienced catering staff can re-create the festive atmosphere and delicious Mexican and grilled seafood specialties almost anywhere. They have catered everything from outdoor fiestas in Houston to the first fajita dinner in Latvia in the Soviet Union.

The growing popularity of Mexican catering has expanded the variety of possibilities from rehearsal dinners and wedding receptions to casino parties, fund-raisers and business receptions as well as bar mitzvahs, baby christenings, family dinners and private birthday parties. Among the latter was a party for 400 honoring author Alfred de Marigny on his 80th birthday.

You can choose dinner selections from the restaurant menu or request that the chef prepare your favorite dish for a catered party.

Mexican food can carry out the fiesta theme at a buffet, brunch, seated dinner or cocktail party. To add to the party atmosphere, the catering manager can arrange for special decorations, strolling mariachis or a salsa band.

Jalapeños has catered events for the Houston Rockets, recruitment parties for Fulbright & Jaworski law firm, monthly business luncheons for Citicorp, and for the Tower Theater for musicians Edgar Winter and Rick Derringer.

Jalapeños catered in the Texas Pavilion for President Bush's thank-you to Houston after the economic summit.

For Charity Players, a fund-raising group, Jalapeños was the setting for a Jalapeño "Jalloween" gala for 600. More frequently, the restaurant is the setting for smaller parties of up to 125 guests. Many clients book the colorful restaurant for private celebrations, but Jalapeños has even catered an office party on a yacht.

Catering Star Attractions

★ Complete party planning — decorations, entertainment and food — coordinated by the catering manager. The host or hostess can relax and leave the details to the staff.

★ On-site catering manager at every function.

★ Well-trained, on-call waiters staff functions of almost any size.

★ Diversified menus. Romero has catered a variety of functions including Italian, Continental, Mexican, Peruvian and Southern cooking. Catering menus available on request.

★ Excellent value — prices start at $8.50 per person (plus tax, delivery and set up, attendants) for a Tex-Mex combination including chicken flautas, enchiladas, Mexican rice and refried beans.

★ A Mexican buffet like that set up weekends in the restaurant makes a great party theme. The menu features enchiladas (including Jalapeños' superb spinach enchiladas), made-to-order omelets, carnitas (bits of pork with condiments wrapped in freshly made flour tortillas), fresh fruit and bunelos, fried pastries.

★ Highest quality food prepared by professional chef. Catering menus and themes vary but one theme prevails — excellent quality food, well prepared and expertly coordinated.

★ Specialties such as Peruvian-style ceviche, stuffed jalapenos, spinach enchiladas, shrimp quesadillas and excellent margaritas.

Spinach Enchiladas

4   (10-ounce) packages frozen chopped
    spinach or 4 bunches fresh spinach,
    cooked
6   teaspoons chopped garlic
1   large onion, chopped (8 ounces)
1   pound fresh mushrooms, cut in halves
2   teaspoons butter
2   slices white bread
    Salt if needed
2   teaspoons white pepper
¼   teaspoon nutmeg
½   teaspoon chili powder
2   eggs
    Mixed Monterey Jack and Cheddar
    cheese
10 to 12 flour tortillas
    Cilantro Cream Sauce (recipe follows)

Make spinach filling. While spinach is
cooking, combine garlic, onion and mushrooms
in food processor, and process to about ¼- to
⅛-inch in size. Saute onion mixture in butter in
non-stick pan until onion is transparent. Remove from heat, and set aside. Drain spinach;
squeeze out excess water.

Make bread crumbs of the bread in food
processor. Add drained spinach, salt, white
pepper, nutmeg, chili powder and eggs.
Process until blended thoroughly. Transfer to
mixing bowl, and stir in 6 tablespoons mixed
Monterey Jack and Cheddar cheese.

Spoon a portion of the filling onto each
flour tortilla, roll up and place in casserole or
rectangular ovenproof dish. Pour Cilantro
Cream Sauce over top and sprinkle liberally
with grated cheese. Heat under broiler until
cheese melts, or reheat in microwave; keep
warm in chafing dish.

Serves 10 to 12.

Jalapeños Seafood-Mexican Cocina & Cantina
2702 Kirby Dr. at Westheimer
Houston, Texas 77098
524-1668

Cilantro Cream Sauce
3   cups heavy (whipping) cream
¼   teaspoon cayenne pepper
1½ teaspoons salt
5   teaspoons cornstarch dissolved in
    cold water
3   cups chopped cilantro leaves

Mix cream, cayenne, salt and a little of the
dissolved cornstarch in a 2-quart saucepan
and heat, stirring, over medium heat until
thickened; sauce should be creamy, but not
runny. Add cilantro. If made ahead, reheat
(can use microwave) before using.

Substitute whole milk for cream; low fat or
part skim cheese for regular.

British Petroleum Yachting Party
for 35

Grilled Shrimp, Quail and Frog Legs
Mexican Rice and Refried Beans
Pico de Gallo
Flan
Margaritas, Sangria and Mexican Beer

Jalapeño "Jalloween"

Deep-Fried Shrimp-Stuffed Jalapenos
Carnitas with Jalapeno-Pineapple Salsa
Chicken Flautas with Molcajete Sauce

Jalapeños

THE HOT SPOT ON KIRBY

Mexican Restaurante
& Cantina

Marthann Masterson-
Gourmet to Go

Marthann Masterson is known for producing lively parties with style and dash. A dedicated caterer who handles events for a demanding and highly discriminating clientele, Masterson has earned a reputation for fun parties where the food sets the mood.

Since she came on the catering scene in 1983, Masterson has done parties for clients as diverse as U.S. Secretary of the Treasury Nicholas Brady, museums and the Rolling Stones.

Her food repertoire is equally varied — from breakfasts or simple picnics of crudites, pate, cheese and fruit to classical Italian and adventurous Southwestern fare.

Brady's luncheon was only one of the events Masterson catered during the 1990 economic summit. She was in charge of the Italian pavilion, one of nine food tents for President Bush's thank-you party for 15,000 volunteers and other summit planners.

Masterson, a board member of the American Institute of Wine and Food and member of the Houston Culinary Guild, also is in charge of the cafe at the Museum of Fine Arts. The menu there features several of her signature salads, sandwiches and some of the most popular specialties sold as gourmet-to-go items at her catering shop.

*Catering office hours at the kitchen-shop are 9 a.m. to 5 p.m. Monday through Friday; an answering service takes calls at other times.

*Catering minimum is six people.

*Schedule catering as early as possible; 24-hour notice requested for weekday catering; notice by Friday morning for weekend catering.

*Delivery fee is $6 to $15. Set-up fee is $15 for most areas of Houston.

*Gourmet to Go specialties may be picked up at the walk-in take-out kitchen-shop, 3821 Farnham, where it merges with Greenbriar just north of the Southwest Freeway.

*Payment can be cash, checks, American Express, MasterCard or Visa.

Star Attractions

★ Full range of catering services.

★ Take-out food for today's gourmet — chic as orzo pasta or homey as egg salad and oatmeal cookies.

★ Distinguished client list including: President George Bush (then vice president) & Funds for America's Future; Dr. and Mrs. Denton Cooley, Robert Mosbacher/Mosbacher Energy, Inc., Shell Oil Corp., CBS Network, The Smithsonian Institution, Mr. and Mrs. A. Robert Abboud, Mr. and Mrs. Alfred Glassell, Andrews & Kurth, Baker & Botts and Vinson & Elkins law firms; Walter Mischer Companies, Houston Olympic Festival and Transco Energy, Inc.

★ Theme parties such as:
Caribbean party for the King of Norway at the Texas Corinthian Yacht Club. The menu included smoked salmon, scallop ceviche and chicken and banana kabobs.

Texas food — ranch-style, Tex-Mex and Gulf Coast seafood or a combination — served on tables covered with red and white star-pattern rugs; fresh fruits, vegetables and wildflowers displayed in baskets.

"The Best Little Whorehouse in Texas" was the theme for a party in Magnolia Ballroom. Actresses dressed as characters in the musical, and the Texas menu featured grilled quail with cilantro pesto, spicy beef tamales, grilled pork tenderloin, fajitas, crudites and spicy Cajun chicken wings.

"Old Woman Who Lived in a Shoe" theme for a 30th birthday party. Invitations featured a caricature of the honoree as the old woman in the shoe with her children, and guests came dressed as their favorite nursery rhyme characters. The menu included Queen Victoria Soup, grilled redfish with lime cilantro sauce, wild rice and orzo, grilled vegetable medley, hot water cornbread and "Blackbird (dewberry) Pie."

With one day's notice, Masterson catered food for the Rolling Stones — crudites, Seafood Cannelloni, Crawfish Quesadillas (which the Stones raved about, she said), beef tenderloin with sauteed baby vegetables, fruit and cheese board.

Party for 150 guests for the Smithsonian Institution at the Museum of Fine Arts. On the menu: Belgian endive in peppercorn sauce with chopped red pepper; red snapper cakes on Boston lettuce with a tomato dill sauce; rare roast beef tenderloin with Madeira mushroom sauce; roasted new potatoes with parsley; green bean bundles, and Lemon Mousse with raspberry Chambord Sauce and chocolate-dipped madeleines.

Informal Christmas Eve soup buffet with three types of soup — pumpkin with almonds, scallop bisque and corn chowder with ancho chilies. Soups were served in demitasse cups and accompanied by a variety of muffins — blue corn, yellow corn muffins with chopped red and green peppers and whole-wheat.

Specialties such as Mediterranean Salad, Sesame Fried Chicken with Honey Mustard Sauce (a best seller), whole roast chicken with garlic and rosemary, whole fish baked in a salt crust, classic chicken salad, Smoked Turkey and Spinach sandwich, smoked pork tenderloin with apple mango chutney.

Economic Summit Luncheon for Financial Ministers
Host: Nicholas Brady, U.S. Secretary of the Treasury
Wortham House, Houston
July 10, 1990

Crawfish Quesadillas

Guacamole Shrimp Nachos

Gulf Coast Crab Cakes

Cayenne Mayonnaise

Rare Roast Beef Tenderloin

Madeira Sauce

*Quail with Baby Vegetables,
Roasted New Potatoes*

*Raspberry Creme Brulee, Fresh Berries and
Raspberry Sauce*

Luncheon Menu Suggestions

CHICKEN

Chicken Parmesan with Fettuccine

*Grilled Chicken and Orzo Pasta with
Wild Rice and Black Beans*

*Sesame Fried Chicken with
Honey Mustard Sauce*

Whole Roasted Rosemary Chicken

Chicken Pot Pie

FISH AND SEAFOOD

Red Snapper Cakes with Tomato Sauce

Old-Fashioned Tuna Casserole

Shell Pasta with Pesto and Shrimp

BEEF AND PORK

Beef Stroganoff

Spaghetti with Meatballs

Pot Roast with Root Vegetables

Beef Pot Pie

Pork Tenderloin with Apple-Pear Chutney

Pork Chops with Apples and Onions

VEGETABLES AND SALADS

Greek Vegetable Salad

Thai Chicken Salad

Mixed Greens with Creamy Basil Dressing

Wild Rice and Orzo Pasta with Black Beans

Sauteed Mixed Vegetables

Peas with Mushrooms

Steamed Broccoli with Lemon Butter

Green Beans with Dill

Creamed Spinach

Mashed Potatoes

Marthann Masterson/Gourmet to Go
3821 Farnham at the Southwest Freeway
Houston, Texas 77098
522-1510

Ruth Meric Catering

Ruth Meric's catering style blends southern hospitality and city sophistication. From breakfast in bed for two to a seated dinner for 125 at the Museum of Fine Arts, Meric creates imaginative menus and mouth-watering food.

She got her start as secretary to a chef at the Royal Sonesta Hotel in New Orleans and worked her way to the kitchen via the front door (hostess at Brennan's of Houston), back of the house (purchasing manager) and front of the house (sales director and assistant general manager).

Through observing and working with such chefs as Paul Prudhomme, Willy Coln of the Sonesta and Mark Cox of Tony's, Meric developed a love of cooking and party planning.

In May, 1983, Noel Hennebery, who had been managing partner of Brennan's, asked her to manage his new restaurant, Charley T's. About two years later, she also took over the kitchen at Charley T's, and that year the restaurant was chosen as one of the 50 best new restaurants in the nation by Gentlemen's Quarterly.

When Charley T's closed in 1988 because of a foreclosure of the building it was in, Meric took her savings and started the catering firm.

She has catered weddings, fund-raisers, a party for 500 for the opening of the IMAX Center at the Museum of Natural Science, a luncheon for two at which Mayor Kathy Whitmire was the honor guest, and a Texas-theme dinner at a private home for the top executive of Mitsubishi during the 1990 economic summit.

Meric has catered parties for many corporate clients and for the Houston Rockets, professional basketball team.

An active member of the International Association of Cooking Professionals and former chairwoman of the Houston Culinary Guild, Meric keeps abreast of professional development by attending workshops and seminars such as the California Wine Festival and Symposium on American Cuisine. She also has traveled throughout Europe and America.

She also does consulting work and food styling for clients including Chantal cookware.

She developed the Classic Lite line of low-fat, low-cholesterol and low-sodium frozen entrees with calorie counts from 200 to 400. The entrees are available at her shop, and several are carried at Rice Epicurean Markets. They range from $4 to $7 and include Fricassee of Cornish Hens with Aromatic Vegetables and Deviled Crab Cakes in Shells.

Star Attractions

★ Can cater a wide variety and sizes of parties from Texas hoe downs to corporate meetings. Custom menus to suit clients' tastes and needs.

★ All items prepared with highest quality fresh ingredients.

★ Located in the Gardens of Bammel Lane, which provides a large glass conservatory that is perfect for parties, private dinners and weddings. Food comes directly from Meric's catering kitchen just a few feet away.

★ Gourmet to Go — Dishes prepared to order with 24-hour advance notice. Order anything for pick-up from brunch to a dinner for a crowd. Hours are 10 a.m. to 7 p.m. Monday through Friday.

★ Evening with the Chef — popular cooking demonstration parties for as many as 10. Varied menus or by special request. Guests help with cooking, then are served a four-course dinner

★ Take-out Classic Lite frozen entrees, a line of more than 20 low-calorie, low-fat, low-sodium, low-cholesterol entrees, of 200 to 400 calories, including Smoked Chicken with Chicken Noodles, Broccoli and Water Chestnuts, Turkey Etouffee with Rice, Roasted Salmon with Fresh Herbs and Spiral Pasta and Grilled Veal Chop with Sun Dried Cherries and

Mushrooms. Ready in five minutes if reheated in the microwave, but may be reheated in a conventional oven.

★ Free home delivery in certain areas when order is for eight or more items.

Creole Corn Chowder

This was a favorite recipe at Charley T's restaurant, and Meric still makes it for catering customers.

- **2 cups each, finely diced: bacon, onion, green bell pepper, red bell pepper and ham**
- **4 cups fresh (or canned) corn kernels**
- **3 cups diced tomato**
- **½ cup tomato juice**
- **1 teaspoon each: dried crushed oregano, basil and thyme leaves**
- **2 teaspoons crushed red pepper**
- **1 teaspoon crushed black pepper**
- **2 cups milk**
- **¼ cup flour**
- **¼ cup oil**
- **2½ cups heavy (whipping) cream**

Saute bacon until crisp in heavy pan. Add onion and peppers and cook until limp. Add ham, corn, tomatoes, juice, oregano, basil, thyme, red and black pepper; simmer 30 minutes. Bring milk to a boil.

Make a roux of flour and oil: Heat oil, whisk in flour, stir until smooth, then simmer over medium-low heat until roux is light brown, about 10 to 20 minutes. Add roux to the corn mixture and mix well. Add milk and simmer 15 to 20 minutes. When ready to serve, add cream and heat through.

Serves 12.

🍎 Substitute 3 cups extra lean ham for bacon and ham; 2 cups skim milk for whole; evaporated skim milk for heavy cream.

Dinner Menus

HOT

Creole Corn Chowder

Grilled Chicken Breast Stuffed with Goat Cheese and Peppers

Southwest Pasta (Linguini with Black Beans, Corn and Peppers)

Cornbread Muffins

Mexican Chocolate Ice Cream with Grand Marnier Oranges

Sugar Cookies

Coffee

Linguini with Crabmeat

Grilled Veal Rib Eye with Shiitakes, Roma Tomatoes and Artichokes

Wild Rice

Mixed Summer Vegetables

Wheat Rolls

Apple Strudel with Heavy Cream

COLD MENUS

Vichyssoise

Pork Tenderloin with Roasted Peppers, Goat Cheese, Pepper Jelly

Chilled Vegetables: Artichokes, Zucchini, Eggplant, Squash, Onion

Angel Hair Pasta

Cornbread Sticks

Charlotte Russe

Cream of Romaine Soup

Cold Poached Salmon with Two Sauces

Fresh Asparagus

Chilled Potatoes

French Bread

Sherry Pound Cake with Fresh Strawberries

Ruth Meric Catering
3004 Philfall-Gardens of Bammel Lane
Houston, Texas 77098
522-1449

Special Helps

Some terms and recipes from restaurant owners and professional chefs may be unfamiliar to the home cook. Here are several that you may see frequently:

Achiote — a yellow seasoning and color, the seeds of the annatto tree. Used in Central, South American, Indian, Mexican and Southwestern cooking.

Ancho chilies — dried poblano peppers.

Capers — the small green berry-like buds of the caper bush used as a condiment or to give piquant flavor to sauces. Usually available bottled or pickled in vinegar.

Chipotle — Dried, smoked red jalapenos.

Chocolate — to melt in microwave: place chocolate in glass dish and melt on medium (50 percent) power, about 1½ to 2 minutes per square, stirring midway through. Chocolate may not look melted; test by stirring to smooth.

Clarified butter — Often used in delicate, fine dishes because it doesn't burn as easily as whole butter. Melt butter (preferably unsalted) over low heat until the foam disappears from top and sediment collects in bottom of pan. Butter should be golden yellow and clear; do not let burn. Pour clear butter off; discard sediment.

Coulis — pureed mixtures of fruits or vegetables.

Cream — when chefs list cream as an ingredient, they usually mean heavy cream (36 percent milkfat).

Heavy cream is usually labeled whipping cream. When whipped, it doubles in volume. Most whipping cream now is ultra-pasteurized for longer shelf life. Better texture and optimum volume are achieved if the cream, bowl and beaters are thoroughly chilled before the cream is beaten.

Some better supermarkets stock heavy whipping cream.

If light cream is specified, look for cream labeled coffee cream or table cream.

Deglaze — Pour off all but a tablespoon or two of accumulated fat from sauteed food. Add stock, water, wine or liquid called for in the recipe and simmer, scraping up browned bits from bottom of pan with a wooden spoon.

End Hunger Network — Many of the hotels and restaurants in this book contribute unused or specially prepared food to the End Hunger Network, a worldwide alliance of private and volunteer organizations committed to ending hunger in the world by the year 2000.

The Houston Chapter sponsors the Red Barrel program of food collection in hundreds of local supermarkets and the End Hunger Loop, which collects food from restaurants and distributes it to area missions and shelters. Call 963-0099 for information.

Herbs — Fresh are preferable if of good quality. The rule of thumb in substituting dried herbs is one to three — one teaspoon dried substituted for three teaspoons fresh.

Zest — thinnest colored part of the peel only, such as lemon or lime zest.

Olive oil — Extra-virgin olive oil is preferred by most chefs because it is the finest quality and has a more delicate flavor. Because it has a low smoking point, it is not suitable for frying as are lower grades. Use extra-virgin olive oil for salad dressings or uncooked dishes.

Less expensive grades such as superfine virgin, virgin or those labeled "pure" are better for everyday use. Store olive oil in a cool, dark place.

Pasta — Make your own or purchase from supermarkets or pasta shops; use fresh or dried. Fresh pasta is best with light, fresh tomato sauces or delicate cream sauces; dried pasta, with heartier long-simmered meat and red sauces.

Fresh pasta takes only 3 to 5 minutes to cook; dried may take as long as 15. Pasta should always be cooked "al dente" which means "firm to the tooth". It should lose its floury taste, but not be hard or mushy.

Do not rinse cooked pasta with cold water unless using pasta for salads or holding it after it is made to serve later. Rinse in cold water or hold in ice water until needed. Plunge strainer of pasta into hot water to revive, then drain and serve. For best quality, hold pasta in cold water no longer than 30 minutes.

Peppers — To roast fresh peppers, rinse and dry, place on baking sheet and broil 4 to 5 inches from heat 5 minutes on each side or until the surface of each pepper is blistered and somewhat blackened. Drop into ice water and let sit for a few minutes; skins will rub off easily.

Other methods: Rub peppers with oil (optional) and grill over mesquite or charcoal, or place on end of long-tined fork and hold over gas burner until charred. Proceed as above to peel.

Handle jalapenos and other hot peppers with care as peppers and fumes can irritate skin and eyes. Wearing rubber gloves is recommended. Removing the walls and seeds of peppers cuts the heat.

Reduce — Cook a mixture down slowly until reduced by half or amount specified. In contemporary cooking, reductions are frequently used to concentrate flavors or thicken sauces instead of thickening with flour or other starches.

Roux — A mixture of flour and fat that is the thickening base for many sauces and soups, particularly Cajun dishes such as gumbo. The usual method is to heat oil until it is at the point of smoking, then to whisk in flour and stir constantly until mixture is a dark mahogany brown, almost black.

Roux requires close attention; it must be stirred or whisked almost constantly for 45 minutes to an hour or it will burn.

Roux is much easier in the microwave. The following method is described by newspaper microwave columnists Ann Steiner and CiCi Williamson in their first book, "Microwave Know-How."

Heat ½ cup each oil and flour in a 4-cup glass measure. Microwave on high power 6 to 7 minutes, stirring every minute after 4 minutes, until a deep brown roux is formed.

Stock — Stocks made on the premises are the rule with chefs and caterers represented in this book, but most realize that busy home cooks will use canned broth and stocks. Unfortunately, canned broths tend to be very salty so choose low-sodium canned broth or buy good quality canned products and adjust salt called for in the recipe.

When making stock at home, use a non-aluminum pan. For clear stock, skim foam and scum off top as it accumulates. Stir as little as possible to prevent clouding. Stock should simmer slowly, not boil. Cool quickly (setting the pan of stock in a container or sink or cold water speeds the process).

Chill, then remove congealed fat from top. Refrigerate or freeze.

Beef or veal stock: Combine 2 to 4 pounds beef bones and meaty soup bones or veal bones and trimmings (brown half the meat) in a saucepot. Add 3 quarts cold water, 8 peppercorns, 1 each onion, carrot and celery rib cut in pieces, 3 whole cloves, 1 bay leaf, 5 sprigs parsley and other desired herbs such as dried thyme.

Bring to a boil and skim off foam. Simmer covered 3 hours, skimming occasionally. Strain stock, cool quickly and refrigerate or freeze. When cold, remove any solid fat that has risen to the top. (Remove fat before freezing.)

Chicken stock: Place 3 pounds bony chicken parts in a stockpot with 3 quarts cold water, a quartered onion stuck with 2 whole cloves, 2 each celery ribs and carrots, 10 peppercorns, 5 sprigs parsley and 1 bay leaf. Cover pot, bring to a boil over medium heat, then reduce heat and simmer stock partially covererd, 2 to 3 hours.

For clear stock, skim off foam and scum on the surface. Add salt to taste after about 1 hour. Strain stock and discard bones and solids. Let cool. Refrigerate or freeze when cool.

Vinegar — Use clear white vinegar unless another type, such as cider, fruit-flavored, rice wine or balsamic vinegar, is specified.

Balsamic vinegar, a dark aged Italian vinegar, is very popular with food professionals and gourmet cooks, especially in salad dressings.

Shopping Guide

Here are some sources for ingredients called for in recipes in "Houston Gourmet Cooks and Caterers."

Better supermarkets carry most items including cilantro (fresh coriander or Chinese parsley), fresh produce such as tomatillos, spices, herbs, puff pastry, imported sauces and fish.

Bakeries such as French Gourmet (three locations) and Paris Bakery (Clear Lake at 515 Bay Area Boulevard) sell puff pastry dough, patty shells and specialty breads; frozen puff pastry can usually be substituted for homemade pastry.

General

Fiesta Marts, 20 locations including the newest store in Deerbrook. Excellent source for fresh produce — 400 to 600 items stocked — baked goods, ethnic foods, specialty foods and imported items from all over the world, especially Mexican, Latin, Chinese, Asian and Middle Eastern. Fiesta stores have the ambiance of an open-air Mexican mercado, which has strolling mariachi musicians and street venders.

Fiesta's largest market, more than 180,000 square feet, is at 20740 Gulf Freeway (I-45 South) at Nasa Road 1. It features a glassed-in hydroponic produce garden, Japanese sushi bar, specialty bakery, coffee-tea bar, exotic fresh and frozen produce from all over the world, prepared take-out foods and fresh seafood market as well as the customary food departments.

The **Jamail Family Market,** 3333 S. Rice Avenue, south of The Galleria area, 621-8030. The market, which opened in May, 1987, is operated by brother and sister, Joe Jamail and Marian Jamail Averyt, and Joe's sons, Jimmy and Larry — part of the family known as "the" gourmet food merchants of Houston.

They pride themselves on stocking the freshest and finest produce, meats, seafood and wines. Selections reflect customers favorites. The gourmet deli specializes in light cuisine including fat-and sodium-reduced entrees and salads.

Jamail Brothers Food Market (Clarence and Edward Jamail), 2110 S. Shepherd, 523-2531. Small market with select merchandise. Personal attention and fine quality are the tradition here.

Kroger, 3665 Highway 6 at Settler's Way in Sugar Land. Opened in May, 1988, this 62,000-square-foot supermarket is an example of the "Power Alley" supermarket concept. Heavy emphasis is placed on specialty perishable items and gourmet foods — a wine steward is in charge of what Kroger boasts is the largest selection of wines in a Texas supermarket, and there are more than 400 varieties of produce including a large section of imported and ethnic items.

In-house fruit and vegetable juice bar; wide selection of cheeses, gourmet cooking oils and vinegars, specialty breads from in-house bakery. Deli includes specialties prepared by in-house chef.

Leibman's Wine & Fine Foods, 14014A Memorial Dr. at Kirkwood, 493-3663. Excellent source for wines, hard-to-find spices such as saffron, large selections of Southwestern ingredients — dried chilies, basil pesto mix, blue corn meal — extra-virgin olive oils, mustards, vinegars (including many fruit-flavored vinegars), rices, pastas, specialty bacons and meats such as pancetta, air-dried beef (Italian brasola and German buenderfleisch) and double smoked bacon, prosciutto, deboned quail, dried mushrooms, mustards (42 varieties), olives, chutneys, condiments, sundried tomatoes (bulk and in oil), creme fraisch and cheeses including Larsen's goat milk cheese from Texas, reduced salt and low-cholesterol cheeses.

Randall's Flagship stores, 41 locations
(the 42nd opens in the fall of 1990) — Flagship stores: 1407 South Voss Road at Woodway; 2586 Weslayan at Bissonnet, Shepherd Square (South Shepherd at Westheimer) and 5219 FM 1960 in Champions. Superior supermarkets featuring imported and locally grown fresh produce, domestic and imported specialty foods, meats and seafood. Will custom-order products on request. Stock no alcoholic beverages.

Rice Epicurean Markets, 3 locations — 4016 San Felipe, 6425 San Felipe and 3102 Kirby Drive. Michael Bove, specialty foods director, and buyers have assembled "boutique" collections of specialty and gourmet foods including Balducci's in New York, pastas, regional and ethnic items, cheeses, wines, meats, seafood, oils, vinegars, chocolates, deli and imported foods. A full kitchen, in-house bakery and specialty butcher provide custom take-out items.

Star attractions: Texas specialty foods, wide assortment of pastas — fresh, dry and frozen; reputation for introducing new and exclusive foods; regular program of demonstrations by top chefs, food personalities and cookbook authors; branch of Methodist Hospital's Institute for Preventive Medicine at the Epicurean Market, 6425 San Felipe. Director is Molly Gee, a registered, licensed dietitian; it features classes in nutrition, weight-loss and heart-healthy cooking.

Richard's Liquors and Fine Wines — 2124 S. Shepherd and several other locations. Richard's was established in 1949 and continues to be one of the city's finest wine and food shops.

Star attractions at larger stores: wines from around the world including great vintages and large selections of French Bordeaux and Burgundies; extensive line of imported and domestic cheeses, extensive line of imported and domestic deli meats including Italian pancetta bacon, prosciutto, Westphalian and Black Forest hams; custom gift baskets; series of wine seminars/tastings; wide selection of specialty Cognacs, brandies, fruit brandies and Scotches.

Spec's Liquor Warehouse & Deli, 2410 Smith Street, and other locations. Impressive selection of wines, liquors and liqueurs, coffee (more than 80 varieties; most roasted in-house), domestic and imported cheeses, spices and seasonings, oils, variety of pastas, preserves, vinegars, sundried tomatoes and several varieties of dried mushrooms.

Whole Foods Market, 2900 S. Shepherd. Imported and/or organically grown fruits and vegetables, sauces, condiments; wide variety of bulk grains and cereals, herbs, spices and seasonings; cheeses including award-winning cheeses from Mozzarella Company of Dallas; natural yogurts, frozen foods, additive-free beef and chicken, baked goods, wines, beers, teas, coffees, healthful frozen entrees, local and regional specialty products including preserves, sauces and cookies.

Chinese, Asian

Various markets in Chinatown east of Main Street around McKinney and St. Emanuel.

Asiatic Import Company, 909 Chartres (227-7979).

Chinatown Market, 1806 Polk Ave. (650-0757).

Diho Market, 9280 Bellaire Blvd. (988-1881). Extensive stock of Chinese and Oriental products, fresh meats, fish, wines, sauces, frozen and prepared items.

Dynasty Supermarket in Dynasty Plaza, 9600 Bellaire (995-4088). Full line supermarket of Oriental and Chinese staples, condiments and hot deli items; fresh fish, wines and beers.

Viet Hoa Supermarket, 8200 Wilcrest at Beechnut (561-8706). Complete supermarket including fish market, produce shop and wide assortment of Asian ingredients.

Nutrition Analysis
*Health Conscious Recipes

	Portion	Calories	Carbohydrates(g)	Protein(g)	Fat(g)	% Fat Calories	Cholesterol(mg)	Sodium(mg)	Diet
* Apple Strudel (Byron Franklin)	1/12	317	56	6	7	20	23	27	4
Artichoke Fritters (Rainbow Lodge)	1/6	815	36	8	73	79	3	397	5
Baby Leaf Greens with Oysters (Jack's)	1/4	789	45	13	63	71	68	396	2
* Modified Recipe	1/4	253	34	10	9	32	34	124	3
Baked Snapper Genovese Style (Rao's)	1/4	694	35	50	39	51	83	420	2
* Modified Recipe	1/4	499	35	50	17	31	83	154	2
Beef ala Scott (Empress of China)	1/4	674	19	47	45	60	279	969	1
Beefsteak Pizzaiola (Carrabba's)	8 oz.	968	12	86	64	60	228	1703	2
* Modified Recipe	4 oz.	321	4	39	16	46	108	340	1
Best Darn Margaritas (How Sweet It Is)	1	146	12	0	0	0	0	3	0
Bistec ala Mexicana (Ninfa's)	6 oz.	752	62	61	29	35	174	2481	10
* Modified Recipe	3 oz.	479	62	37	10	18	71	180	10
* Broth-Cooked Shredded Pork (Empress of China)	1/2	288	9	33	14	46	105	846	0
* Modified Recipe	1/2	225	5	33	8	32	105	227	0
Candied Ancho Chile Butter (Adam's Mark)	1	640	24	1	62	85	166	964	0
Caponata (Carrabba's)	1/2 cup	105	9	2	8	63	1	238	3
* Modified Recipe	1/2 cup	75	9	2	4	49	1	238	3
Char Su Beef Tenderloin (Four Seasons)	1/4	632	46	56	25	35	145	1158	8
* Modified Recipe	1/4	486	46	40	16	30	98	731	8
Chicken Breast Santa Fe (Rainbow Lodge)	1/4	567	9	51	37	58	84	279	1
* Modified Recipe	1/4	317	8	39	13	39	84	230	1
* Chicken Tetrazzini (Melange)	1 cup	300	18	40	9	27	100	367	1
Chicken with Mustard (LaTour d'Argent)	1/4	363	2	55	14	36	172	203	1
* Modified Recipe	1/4	332	2	55	10	29	157	203	1
Chili con Queso (Ninfa's)	1/2 cup	304	4	17	25	72	76	1088	0
Chorizo (Ninfa's)	8 oz.	701	3	58	49	65	206	682	0
* Modified Recipe	4 oz.	193	1	33	6	27	105	344	0
Cold Cream of Asparagus Soup (La Tour d'Argent)	1/2	960	15	9	100	90	336	140	3
* Modified Recipe	1/2	305	37	23	8	24	10	306	3
Crawfish Tails (Backstreet/Prego)	1	1786	52	87	138	69	617	3258	1
* Modified Recipe	1	825	72	77	25	27	256	1428	1
Creole Corn Chowder (Ruth Meric)	1/12	367	23	10	28	65	80	479	3
* Modified Recipe	1/12	218	26	16	7	22	13	524	3
* Curried Yogurt Sauce (Rainbow Lodge)	1/6	102	22	5	0	4	1	114	4
East/West Salad (JAGS)	1 cup	374	48	7	19	44	0	12	10
* Modified Recipe	1 cup	290	47	6	10	30	0	12	9
Eggplant (Empress of China)	1/4	475	40	10	31	58	18	684	7
Empress Barbecued Spareribs	1/2	931	7	66	69	68	274	968	0
English Trifle (Post Oak Grill)	1/16	724	63	9	46	57	282	143	1
* Fettuccine Cavatore	1/4	387	40	28	13	30	258	307	3
Five Onion Soup (Adam's Mark)	1/4	397	27	21	23	52	41	1296	2
* Modified Recipe	1/4	201	27	10	7	29	9	860	2
Flan (Ninfa's)	1/24	510	76	14	17	30	243	20	0
Gazpacho Blanca (Melange)	1/6	268	10	5	24	81	51	776	2
* Modified Recipe	1/6	85	14	7	0	4	2	801	2
Gazpacho Rio Grande (JAGS)	1/6	156	13	3	12	64	6	421	4
* Modified Recipe	1/6	68	12	2	3	32	0	412	3
Gingered Chicken (Calypso)	8 oz.	654	53	63	21	29	168	243	4
* Modified Recipe	3.5 oz.	327	27	31	10	28	84	122	2
Ginger Marinade (Melange)	1/8	149	20	3	0	0	0	2116	0
* Modified Recipe	1/8	149	20	3	0	0	0	1034	0
Glazed Prawns (Empress of China)	1/2	695	12	37	56	73	332	1318	1
* Modified Recipe	1/2	237	12	37	4	30	332	699	1
Gloria's Chicken (Melange)	1/8	428	21	28	25	54	99	815	1
* Modified Recipe	1/8	321	12	28	17	48	84	522	1
Grilled Baby Leg of Lamb (Jackson)	1/10	576	4	47	41	65	169	228	0
Grilled Tiger Prawns (Jack's)	1/4	293	24	28	11	33	178	756	8
* Modified Recipe	1/4	220	24	24	5	19	166	576	8
Hickory Smoked Tomato Sauce (Prego)	1 cup	91	9	2	6	55	16	106	2
* Modified Recipe	1 cup	41	9	2	0	7	0	14	2
* Hill Country Peach Snow (Adam's Mark)	1 cup	354	83	1	5	11	16	7	4
Jackson Hicks' New Potato Salad	1/16	337	56	5	11	29	8	581	3
* Modified Recipe	1/16	302	51	5	9	28	10	306	3
Jalapeno Ice Cream (Adam's Mark)	1 cup	508	52	10	31	53	309	111	0
Jerk Pork (Calypso)	1/4	566	17	67	25	40	210	232	1
* Modified Recipe	1/4	298	17	35	10	30	105	157	1
Kahlua Banana Colada (Calypso)	1	395	42	3	13	30	22	28	1
Lemon Meringue Tart (Four Seasons)	1/8	706	71	11	42	54	185	902	2

Nutrition Analysis

*Health Conscious Recipes

Recipe	Portion	Calories	Carbohydrates(g)	Protein(g)	Fat(g)	% Fat Calories	Cholesterol(mg)	Sodium(mg)	Dietary Fiber(g)
Lone Star Polenta (Adam's Mark)	⅙	200	17	5	12	55	102	298	1
* Modified Recipe	⅙	142	18	5	5	34	2	291	1
*Mahi Baked in Paper (Jack's)	¼	261	22	26	8	27	55	371	3
*Medallions of Venison (Rainbow Lodge)	6 oz.	378	33	51	4	9	0	144	1
* Modified Recipe	4 oz.	274	28	34	3	9	0	100	1
Nanaimo Bars (How Sweet It Is)	1/36	160	19	2	9	48	20	110	1
Osso Buco (Rao's)	⅓	466	17	25	33	63	87	410	2
* Modified Recipe	⅓	307	17	25	14	43	87	410	2
Pasta alla Vodka (Rao's)	¼	677	39	18	51	67	156	1078	2
* Modified Recipe	¼	329	42	16	10	29	12	481	2
Pasta and Shrimp Salad (Taste of Texas)	¼	430	25	32	22	46	401	496	2
* Modified Recipe	¼	265	23	21	10	33	176	279	2
Pasta Frittata (Carrabba's)	⅙	497	57	21	20	37	344	622	3
* Modified Recipe	⅙	440	57	25	12	24	217	317	3
Peanut Butter Pie (Calypso)	⅛	573	54	11	37	58	130	311	2
Pecan Pie (Taste of Texas)	⅛	670	65	6	45	58	142	622	1
Pecan Wood-Grilled Lamb Loin (Jack's)	¼	846	41	28	65	68	182	476	1
* Modified Recipe	¼	554	42	34	29	46	77	592	1
Penne Mary Raia (Carrabba's)	⅙	1065	64	28	79	66	308	1346	1
* Modified Recipe	⅙	554	69	26	19	31	96	674	1
Peperonata (Cavatore's)	¼	296	7	1	27	88	0	111	3
* Modified Recipe	¼	155	18	6	7	39	0	205	3
Peppermint Cream (A Fare Extraordinaire)	½ Cup	137	12	5	8	50	231	54	0
Praline Spice Cake (Melange)	1/16	509	69	4	26	44	89	210	1
Pureed Bean Soup with Pasta (Rao's)	¼	495	44	12	32	56	0	318	6
* Modified Recipe	¼	306	44	12	32	56	0	318	6
Ratatouille (Atchafalaya)	½ Cup	142	11	2	11	64	0	502	3
* Modified Recipe	½ Cup	82	11	2	4	40	0	502	3
*Risotto Milanese (Rao's)	¼	237	41	4	7	25	8	32	1
Roast Chicken Breast (Prego)	⅙	457	1	54	25	51	161	185	0
* Modified Recipe	1	378	1	54	16	40	161	185	0
*Roast Corn and Shrimp Salad (Backstreet)	1	466	59	41	10	18	246	599	16
Roast Prime Rib (Taste of Texas)	10 oz.	1455	12	81	19	74	332	5119	2
Sauteed Baby Shrimp (Fu's Garden)	¼	366	10	28	24	58	221	805	2
Sauteed Green Beans (Fu's Garden)	¼	105	10	4	8	48	8	866	1
Sauteed Chicken (Fu's Garden)	¼	388	8	37	22	53	96	634	1
Scallion Crepes (A Fare Extraordinaire)	1/20	61	6	3	3	44	39	143	0
*Scallops (Cavatore)	½	308	16	30	13	38	87	587	0
Shrimp Gratin (LaTour d'Argent)	½	421	6	36	28	60	259	548	1
* Modified Recipe	½	235	8	30	9	35	194	516	1
Shrimp Tampico (Post Oak Grill)	⅛	540	52	23	27	44	197	317	2
* Modified Recipe	⅛	440	52	23	15	31	166	201	2
Smoked Texas Tenderloin (Adam's Mark)	8 oz.	945	1	65	75	72	191	144	1
* Modified Recipe	4 oz.	236	1	32	11	41	95	72	1
Sour Cherry Relish (A Fare Extraordinaire)	⅒	87	19	7	2	18	0	1	1
South Texas Tenderloin (Taste of Texas)	¼	780	6	61	57	66	126	804	1
* Modified Recipe	¼	323	6	40	15	43	111	206	1
Southern Comfort Pecan Pie (Adam's Mark)	⅛	520	68	5	25	43	23	286	1
Spinach Enchiladas (Jalapeños)	1/12	488	32	14	31	60	93	528	4
* Modified Recipe	1/12	261	33	15	9	30	8	507	4
*Spinach Soup (Cavatore)	1 cup	61	4	8	2	20	5	233	3
*Steamed Salmon (Fu's Garden)	½	320	12	42	11	31	70	622	3
Sweet Potato Pecan Pie (Atchafalaya)	⅒	420	49	5	23	49	98	334	2
*Swordfish San Angelo (Rainbow Lodge)	¼	366	25	45	9	24	86	204	3
Tenderloin Emerson (Post Oak Grill)	8 oz.	862	17	80	54	56	223	543	4
* Modified Recipe	4 oz.	339	7	38	18	47	99	170	2
*Texas Caviar (Taste of Texas)	⅛	52	9	4	1	10	0	161	2
Texas Gulf Shrimp Remoulade (Jackson)	⅙	268	10	24	14	49	232	565	0
* Modified Recipe	⅙	168	2	24	7	37	228	288	0
Texas Pecan Chocolate Mousse Cake (Jackson)	1/16	642	87	6	31	43	47	294	0
Tomatoes Manfred With Crab (Post Oak Grill)	⅙	845	18	31	74	77	62	1407	5
* Modified Recipe	⅙	284	18	31	11	33	62	1407	5
Torte Melange	⅒	383	19	27	22	52	90	981	2
* Modified Recipe	⅒	249	18	19	11	40	48	802	2
Trout Meuniere (Post Oak Grill)	⅙	583	17	45	36	57	184	569	1
* Modified Recipe	⅙	310	17	40	9	27	62	149	1
Veal Scallops Armagnac (LaTour d'Argent)	¼	471	5	32	35	67	188	219	1
* Modified Recipe	¼	320	8	34	11	32	164	152	1
Veal Milanese (Cavatore)	6 oz.	618	10	54	38	57	488	688	0
* Modified Recipe	3 oz.	232	6	26	11	43	94	183	0

Index

Who's Who **HOUSTON GOURMET** Cooks & Caterers

1. Ann Criswell – Food Editor
   Houston Chronicle
2. Jackson Hicks – JAGS -
   Jackson & Company
3. Richard Kaplan – Acute Catering
4. Doreen Kaplan – Acute Catering
5. Ninfa Lorenzo – Ninfa's-Atchafalaya
6. Jill Roman – How Sweet It Is
7. Peter Zimmer – Jack's on Woodway
8. Sonny Lahham – La Tour d'Argent
9. Johnny Carrabba – Carrabba's

10. George Fu – Fu's Garden
11. Ruth Meric – Ruth Meric Catering
12. Neil Doherty – Adam's Mark
13. Marthann Masterson – Marthann
    Masterson Gourmet To Go & Catering
14. Manfred Jachmich – Post Oak Grill
15. Karen Lerner – A Fare Extraordinare
16. Peter Rosenberg – DELICATEXAS
17. Rosemary Rosenberg – DELICATEXAS
18. Scott Chen – Empress of China
19. John Watt – Backsteet - Prego

20. Tim McGann – Calypso
21. Michael Sadek – Cavatore
22. Edd Hendee – Taste of Texas
23. Robert McGrath – Four Seasons
24. Sharon Graham – Melange Catering
    & Gourmet To Go
25. Linda West – Melange Catering &
    Gourmet To Go
26. Chris Goad – Acute Catering
27. Fran Fauntleroy – Publisher
28. Fruit Baskets & Balloons – Rice
    Epicurean Market

HOUSTON GOURMET Cooks & Caterers

Order a book for
a friend.
A Perfect Gift

Order Form

For additional copies of this cookbook contact:
HOUSTON GOURMET
2 Pine Forest
Houston, Texas 77056

Please mail me _____ copies of your **HOUSTON GOURMET** Cooks & Caterers at $14.95 per copy plus $2.00 handling and postage per book. Texas residents, also add applicable state sales tax. Enclosed is my check or money order for $ _____ .

Mail books to:

Name _____

Address _____

City/State _____ Zip _____

Other Books Available

___ **HOUSTON GOURMET COOKS 2**
A Collection of Recipes from
21 of Houston's Most Creative
Restaurants. $12.95

___ **HOUSTON GOURMET 1990**
A Menu Guide to Fine Dining
with "Healthy Eating Tips" $8.95

Please include $2.00 per book for handling & postage. Texas residents, also add applicable state sales tax.

Enclosed is my check or money order for
$ _____ . Mail books to:

Name _____

Address _____

City/State _____ Zip _____